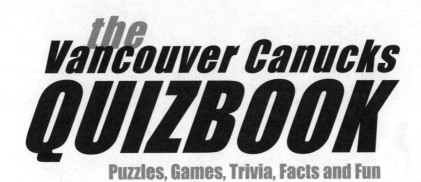

# the Vancouver Canucks QUIZBOOK

## Puzzles, Games, Trivia, Facts and Fun

# The Puzzling Sports Institute

NIGHTWOOD EDITIONS

Copyright © 2010 Puzzling Sports Institute
Second edition revised and updated © 2012

**Nightwood Editions**
Box 1779, Gibsons, BC
V0N 1V0
www.nightwoodeditions.com

All information current as of September 2012.

**Library and Archives Canada Cataloguing in Publication**

    The Vancouver Canucks quizbook / Puzzling Sports Institute, Jesse Ross.—Updated ed.

ISBN 978-0-88971-280-5

    1. Vancouver Canucks (Hockey team)—Miscellanea.
I. Ross, Jesse, 1986– II. Puzzling Sports Institute

GV848.V35V35 2012       796.962'640971133     C2012-903825-3

*Thanks to Ruth, Julian, Kristian, Nathan, Mike and Darnell.*
*Go Canucks Go!*

# Contents

# The Team

28 current and recent Canuck players are listed below. Beside each player write the team he played for before joining Vancouver. If he hasn't played with anyone else, just write 'Van.' Next, write down each player's home country. Good luck!

| Player | Team | Country |
|---|---|---|
| 1) Andrew Alberts | | |
| 2) Keith Ballard | | |
| 3) Kevin Bieksa | | |
| 4) Alexandre Burrows | | |
| 5) David Booth | | |
| 6) Alexander Edler | | |
| 7) Chris Higgins | | |
| 8) Chris Tanev | | |
| 9) Dan Hamhuis | | |
| 10) Jannik Hansen | | |
| 11) Maxim Lapierre | | |
| 12) Victor Oreskovich | | |
| 13) Ryan Kesler | | |

• • • • • • • • • • • • • • • • • • •

*The tall and short of it: the tallest Canuck player in history was 6'7" Chris McAllister, who stood well over a foot taller than the shortest player, 5'5" Bobby Lalonde.*

| Player | Team | Country |
|---|---|---|
| 14) Roberto Luongo | _____ | _____ |
| 15) Manny Malhotra | _____ | _____ |
| 16) Byron Bitz | _____ | _____ |
| 17) Nicklas Jensen | _____ | _____ |
| 18) Cody Hodgson | _____ | _____ |
| 19) Mason Raymond | _____ | _____ |
| 20) Aaron Rome | _____ | _____ |
| 21) Zack Kassian | _____ | _____ |
| 22) Sami Salo | _____ | _____ |
| 23) Aaron Volpatti | _____ | _____ |
| 24) Cory Schneider | _____ | _____ |
| 25) Daniel Sedin | _____ | _____ |
| 26) Henrik Sedin | _____ | _____ |
| 27) Jordan Schroeder | _____ | _____ |
| 28) Brendan Gaunce | _____ | _____ |

• • • • • • • • • • • • • • • • • • •

*Since the lockout in 2004–05, the Canucks have posted an excellent 66–27–1 record against Eastern Conference teams.*

# Around the Rink

The last names of 14 Canucks are listed. Fill their first names into the grid below, beginning with #1 in the upper left corner. Follow the arrows as you work around – the puzzle winds from the outside into the centre. The last letter from the first name forms the first letter from the second name, and so on.

| 1 | | | | 2 | | |
|---|---|---|---|---|---|---|
| | 8 | | | | 9 | 3 |
| 7 | 12 | | 13 | | | |
| | | | | | | |
| | | | 14 | | | |
| 6 | | 11 | | | 10 | |
| | | 5 | | | 4 | |

| | | |
|---|---|---|
| **1)** Lumme | **6)** Belland | **11)** Bernier |
| **2)** Larionov | **7)** Bourdon | **12)** Tikkanen |
| **3)** Brodeur | **8)** Ronning | **13)** Chubarov |
| **4)** Scatchard | **9)** Fedorov | **14)** Sundin |
| **5)** Oberg | **10)** Courtnall | |

*From October 31, 1970 through January 27, 1976 the Canucks could not beat Montreal, a record winless streak of 30 games. Flipping the tables, the longest unbeaten streak for the Canucks is 13 straight against LA in the mid-90s.*

# Draft Day

1) In '89, the Canucks selected 12 players. Only one, Pavel Bure, played a game with the Nucks. Which round was he selected?
   A) Sixth round, 113th overall
   B) First round, 3rd overall
   C) Second round, 33rd overall

2) In '00, the Canucks selected Nathan Smith 25th overall, ahead of...
   A) Brad Boyes, Niklas Kronwall and Ilya Bryzgalov
   B) Mark Stuart, Alexander Frolov and Matthew Lombardi
   C) Scott Hannan, Brendan Morrow and Marian Hossa

3) Picking 2nd overall in '91, Jagr, Tkachuk and Brodeur were passed on for whom?
   A) Jason Herter
   B) Alek Stojanov
   C) Petr Nedved

4) In '92, Libor Polasek (0 NHL GP) was selected 21st overall, ahead of...
   A) Martin Straka, Jason Smith and Chris Osgood
   B) Nikolai Khabibulin, Mike Peca and Mattias Norstrom
   C) Todd Bertuzzi, Saku Koivu and Bryan McCabe

5) In '96, Derek Morris, Marco Sturm and Daniel Briere were passed on for whom?
   A) Harold Druken
   B) Josh Holden
   C) Ryan Bonni

6) Which group of three players were selected by Vancouver at the 2011 Entry Draft?
   A) David Hoznik, Nicklas Blomstrand and Joseph Labate
   B) Steve Pinizzotto, Mike Mancari and Nicklas Jensen
   C) Patrick McNally, Adam Polasek and Alex Friesen

· · · · · · · · · · · · · · · · · · · · · ·

**Q:** *The Canucks have had 13 captains in their history. How many can you name?*

# '70s, '80s, '90s or '00s

Do you know if each event happened in the 1970s, 1980s, 1990s or 2000s?
If you want more of a challenge, try to guess the exact year.

1) The Canucks open the season against Anaheim in Tokyo, Japan. _____

2) Canucks are moved from the Pacific to the Northwest Division. _____

3) Canucks are moved from the Smythe Division in the Campbell Conference to the Pacific Division in the Western Conference. _____

4) After missing the playoffs four straight years, the Nucks make it only to be swept by Colorado. _____

5) GM Place opens, replacing the old Coliseum. _____

6) A Canuck player wins an individual NHL award for the first time. _____

7) Canucks win the sixth-longest game in NHL history. _____

8) Trevor Linden returns to Vancouver after playing for three other teams. _____

9) Canucks win their division for the first time. _____

10) Canucks advance past second round for the first time. _____

11) Canucks record over 100 points in one season for the first time. _____

12) "Iron Mike" Keenan gets fired. _____

13) Roberto Luongo is born. _____

14) Canucks set team record of six straight playoff appearances. _____

15) Canucks sweep a playoff series for the first time. _____

• • • • • • • • • • • • • • • •

**Q:** *Which former Canuck is a member of the Triple Gold Club, having won the World Championships, the Stanley Cup and an Olympic Gold?*

# Nicknames

Can you match up all these Canucks with their nicknames?

| | |
|---|---|
| Mayday | Jim Sandlak |
| Russian Rocket | Kevin Bieksa |
| Steamer | Jeff Cowan |
| Bloodbank | Pavel Bure |
| The Brabarian | Mark Messier |
| Captain Canuck | Curtis Sanford |
| Captain Kirk | Garth Butcher |
| Frankenswede | Brad May |
| The Moose | Willie Mitchell |
| Crouton | Vladimir Krutov |
| Jovocop | Mats Sundin |
| The Sandman | Roberto Luongo |
| The Strangler | Wade Brookbank |
| The House | Kirk McLean |
| Juice | Ed Jovanovski |
| Bill Pickle | Stan Smyl |
| Bobby Lou | Trevor Linden |

. . . . . . . . . . . . . . . . . .

**Q:** *More nicknames:* 1) *Alexander the Great*  2) *Backup Bob*
3) *Big Bert*  4) *King Richard*  5) *The Ripper*  6) *CoHo*  7) *BMO*

# Opening Night

Fill in the grid by answering all the clues.

**Across**
1) Young ex-Canuck troubled with back injuries (last name)
5) Last name of retired #12
9) Bure played in this *city* after leaving Vancouver
10) These men caused a stir beside the penalty box at home games in 10–11
11) First name shared by ex-Canucks' Tannahill, Kozak and Lever
12) First name shared by ex-Canucks' Bouck and Moss
16) Last name of feared Canuck fighter
19) Canucks' "sister team" (joined league at same time)
21) This team eliminated Vancouver in '83, '84, '89 and '04
22) '12 First round playoff opponent
23) Vancouver team that played for the Cup five different times
26) Fans chanted this name of Canuck who played from 74–84 and 88–90
28) Once called a sister
30) Ex-Canuck who stylishly ended longest shootout in history in '05 (last name)
32) Canucks had three of these captains in 2009–10

**Down**
1) Broadcaster who clearly favours one team
2) How the player in 1 Across was acquired
3) All-Star Weekend and the Canucks both have this kind of competition
4) Took over from the NHA in 1917
6) First name of ex-Canuck who won the Jack Adams in '95
7) First main Sedin linemate (first name)
8) _____ Boudrias (led Canucks in scoring four of first five seasons)
13) Last name of famous Canuck broadcaster who was inducted into Canadian Broadcast Hall of Fame in 2002
14) Rogers Arena: 800 _____ Way
15) AKA Greg (as in Adams)
17) Canucks _____ Children's Hospice
18) Last name of retired Canuck with low 26.3 scoring % in shootouts (5 for 19)
20) Brandon _____ (diminutive centre with 23 games between '02 and '07)
23) Former farm team, before they became the Wolves
24) _____ Stanley
25) Length (in years) of Luongo's first contract with Canucks
27) A city in Europe, or a 2011 Canuck
29) Behind the keeper
31) Bad way to lose a fight

• • • • • • • • • • • • • • • • • •

*Mark Messier (who named an award after this guy, anyway?) had an atrocious plus/minus of −35 over three years (207 games) with the club. His career total is +210.*

**Q:** *Five Canucks received at least one vote for the Lady Byng Trophy (gentlemanly play) in 2011–12. Who were they?*

# A Numbers Game

Using the numbers in the box below, can you fill in all these clues about the Canucks?
Cross out the numbers as you go. Each is only used once.

1) # of NHL seasons played (including 2011–12) _____

2) # of playoff appearances _____

3) # of playoff series wins _____

4) # of total playoff games _____

5) Record # of goals scored in one season (1992–93) _____

6) Lowest # of goals scored in one (non-lockout) season (1998–99) _____

7) Record # of points earned in one season (2010–11) _____

8) Lowest # of points earned in one (non-lockout) season (1971–72) _____

9) Record # of PIMs in one season (1992–93) _____

10) Lowest # of PIMs in one season (1972–73) _____

11) Record unbeaten streak at home (set in 1992–93) _____

12) # of consecutive home sellouts before start of 2012–13 season _____

13) Capacity at Rogers Arena _____

14) Capacity at Pacific Coliseum _____

15) Record TV viewers for '12 rematch against Boston on Sportsnet Pacific _____

16) Record TV viewers for one '12 Leafs game on Sportsnet Ontario _____

17) CBC viewers for Game 6 between New Jersey and Los Angeles _____

18) CBC viewers for Game 7 between Boston and Vancouver _____

| | | | | |
|---|---|---|---|---|
| 16 | 48 | 346 | 16,281 | |
| 18 | 117 | 406 | 18,860 | 3,133,000 |
| 25 | 192 | 943 | 746,900 | 8,700,000 |
| 41 | 219 | 2,326 | 1,050,000 | |

**Q:** *Which Canuck was the cover athlete for NHL 2K11?*

# Your Choice

1) Who is longest-serving captain in Canucks history, with eight full seasons?
   A) Markus Naslund
   B) Trevor Linden
   C) Stan Smyl
   D) None of the above (no one has served for eight full seasons)

2) The Canucks' franchise record for the two fastest goals is:
   A) 6 seconds (Greg Adams and Cliff Ronning against the Islanders in '92)
   B) 4 seconds (Daniel Sedin and Ryan Kesler against the Ducks in '07)
   C) 5 seconds (Trent Klatt and Andrew Cassels against the Oilers in '01)

3) Which Canuck famously put a visiting Blue through the home glass?
   A) Harold Snepsts
   B) Trevor Linden
   C) Todd Bertuzzi
   D) Mattias Ohlund

4) Of the Canucks' 41 seasons, how many times have they posted a winning record?
   A) 17
   B) 19
   C) 23
   D) 26

5) What did the Canucks NOT do at home on Boxing Day between 1973 and 2009?
   A) Play a game
   B) Win a game
   C) Lose a game

• • • • • • • • • • • • • • • • • • • •

*With only 23 games played, Mikael Samuelsson is tied for 14th in all-time playoff goals for Vancouver, with nine. Daniel Sedin tops active players with 23 (good for fifth), while Linden and Bure are tied at the top with 34 goals each.*

**6)** How many times have the Canucks won the Northwest Division?

A) 6

B) 7

C) 10

D) 11

**7)** Who was named the Canucks' "Most Exciting Player" from 2008 through 2010, before Ryan Kesler stole it away in 2011?

A) The Sedins

B) Alex Burrows

C) Roberto Luongo

D) Mason Raymond

**8)** Which team do the Sedins have the most combined points against (131), through 2011–12?

A) Edmonton

B) Colorado

C) Calgary

D) Minnesota

**9)** Who was suspended eight games in 2008 for stomping on Ryan Kesler's foot?

A) Chris Pronger

B) Chris Simon

C) Andrew Ladd

D) Steve Downie

**10)** The 2010–11 Canucks led the league in...

A) Goals for (262)

B) Goals against (185)

C) Road wins (27)

D) All of the above

• • • • • • • • • • • • • • • • • • •

*None of Alex Burrows' 28 goals in 2008–09 came on the power play,
the most "power play-less" goals of anyone in the league.*

# The Run

For the second time in franchise history, the 2011 Vancouver Canucks came within one game of hoisting Lord Stanley. Can you fill in which playoff opponent each of these important events happened against?

1) Alex Burrows scores 11 seconds into overtime. _____

2) Kevin Bieksa gets into a fight with an assistant captain. _____

3) Alex Burrows supposedly bites a finger. _____

4) The Canucks win game one 1–0 on a last-minute goal. _____

5) The Canucks lose three in a row. _____

6) The stanchion helps out Kevin Bieksa. _____

7) The Canucks play double-OT for the first time. _____

8) The Canucks win a series on the road. _____

9) Cory Schneider starts a game. _____

10) The Canucks allow seven PP goals on 18 chances. _____

11) A Canuck gets suspended. _____

12) Luongo registers two 1–0 shutouts in the same round. _____

13) Mason Raymond gets injured, ending his playoffs. _____

14) Mikael Samuelsson scores a game-winner, his only goal of the playoffs.

_____

• • • • • • • • • • • • • • • • •

*Before being traded from Florida, Victor Oreskovich briefly retired from hockey, and landed a summer job selling women's shoes at a mall in Notre Dame.*

# SudoClue

Answer the clues below, corresponding to their locations in the grid on the following page. Each clue is answered with a jersey #, and that number goes into the four locations listed in brackets. If a player's # is 16, his "first #" is 1 and his "second #" is 6. This is a sudoku grid, meaning each row, column and 3x3 grid must have the numbers 1–9 in it only once each. After you've filled in the clues, you'll need to complete the grid according to this rule. Player numbers refer to time in Vancouver. We've filled in a few numbers to start you off.

1) Roberto Luongo's #  [C1, D9, F3, G4]

2) Mattias Ohlund's #  [B6, C9, G8, I3]

3) Zack Kassian's #  [C5, E2, G7, I1]

4) Cory Schneider's second #  [A2, D8, E1, G3]

5) Alex Mogilny & Fedor Fedorov are the only two Canucks to have a jersey beginning with this #  [A6, B8, E7, F5]

6) Alex Auld, Cory Schneider and Richard Brodeur's first #  [A5, B7, D2, G1]

7) Keith Ballard's #  [C7, D6, G2, I9]

8) Markus Naslund's second #  [B3, D4, F8, H6]

9) One of Gino Odjick's #'s during his first NHL game (he had to switch his jersey because of Super Mario)  [B1, C8, E3, H9]

10) One of Anson Carter's #'s (who is one of only three players to have a jersey beginning with this #)  [B2, D3, F4, I8]

11) Christian Ehrhoff and Marc-Andre Gragnani's #  [C4, F6, H7, I5]

12) Ryan Kesler's second #  [B4, E8, F1, H5]

•   •   •   •   •   •   •   •   •   •   •   •   •   •   •   •

*The Canucks are 22–25 all-time when facing elimination in the playoffs.*

|   | 1 | 2 | 3 | 4 | 5 | 6 | 7 | 8 | 9 |
|---|---|---|---|---|---|---|---|---|---|
| A |   |   | 4 |   |   |   |   |   | 9 |
| B |   |   |   |   |   |   |   |   |   |
| C |   |   |   |   |   |   |   |   |   |
| D |   |   |   |   |   |   |   |   |   |
| E |   |   |   |   | 2 |   |   |   | 7 |
| F |   |   |   |   |   |   |   |   |   |
| G |   |   |   |   |   |   |   |   |   |
| H |   |   | 8 |   |   |   |   |   |   |
| I |   |   |   |   |   |   | 1 |   |   |

· · · · · · · · · · · · · · · · · · · ·

*Not counting Ryan Kesler, the 21 players drafted by the Canucks in 2002 and 2003 have played a combined 19 NHL games.*

# First Round Search

The last names of 21 first-round Vancouver draft picks are hidden below, going back to '86. As a bonus, put a mark beside every player who actually played a game for Vancouver through the 2010–11 season, and then put a different mark beside each player with 100+ NHL games through 2010–11.

| H | E | R | T | E | R | E | N | B | A | R | G |
|---|---|---|---|---|---|---|---|---|---|---|---|
| P | S | T | O | V | O | N | A | J | O | T | S |
| B | O | U | R | D | O | N | L | H | R | N | E |
| W | N | L | E | H | E | R | L | R | E | I | D |
| O | I | J | A | C | O | U | E | D | L | H | R |
| O | D | L | O | S | N | D | V | J | S | O | E |
| D | E | E | S | D | E | E | G | W | E | L | G |
| L | S | T | W | O | D | K | R | S | K | D | R |
| E | V | I | R | V | N | K | L | E | O | E | E |
| Y | Y | H | S | M | I | T | H | Y | F | N | B |
| H | C | W | K | A | L | N | E | L | L | A | M |
| S | C | H | N | E | I | D | E | R | U | M | U |

| | | |
|---|---|---|
| Bryan ALLEN | Ryan KESLER | Daniel & Henrik SEDIN |
| Luc BOURDON | Trevor LINDEN | Nathan SMITH |
| Brad FERENCE | Petr NEDVED | Alek STOJANOV |
| Michael GRABNER | Mattias OHLUND | R.J. UMBERGER |
| Jason HERTER | Libor POLASEK | Patrick WHITE |
| Cody HODGSON | Cory SCHNEIDER | Mike WILSON |
| Josh HOLDEN | Jordan SCHROEDER | Dan WOODLEY |

• • • • • • • • • • • • • • • • • • • • •

**Q:** *As members of the Canucks, one player appeared five times at the All-Star Game, one four times, and three have appeared three times. Can you name all five players?*

# Down the Centre

Each of these random rows of letters is hiding the full name of a Canuck centreman. Fill in the one missing letter in the centre to reveal each name.
How quickly can you get to the bottom?

**1)** R O B R E N D A ___ M O R R I S O N

**2)** A L E M I K E R ___ A N K E S L E R

**3)** A R T E M C H U ___ A R O V I C H E

**4)** T S C O D Y H O ___ G S O N E R A Y

**5)** E S C O T T H O ___ A S G R A D I N

**6)** A L T I M A R K ___ E S S I E R N T

**7)** E T H A R O L D ___ R U K E N I N G

**8)** A N D R E W C A ___ S E L S O N O V

**9)** T O M I K E S I ___ L I N G E R D E

**10)** E B A R R Y P E ___ E R S O N E T S

**11)** V I G O R L A R ___ O N O V A N E Y

**12)** J O N A T H A N ___ A F A Y E T T E

**13)** C A M D A V E S ___ A T C H A R D S

**14)** S K Y L E W E L ___ W O O D E N G A

**15)** A M A N N Y M A ___ H O T R A N S E

**16)** A M A X I M L A ___ I E R R E T S E

• • • • • • • • • • • • • • • • • • •

**Q:** *The Canucks have played in four different divisions. Can you name them all?*

# Path to the Big Leagues

Can you figure out which Canuck these clues point towards?

1) Drafted 13th-overall in 2009, this Canadian listed Todd Bertuzzi as his favourite player growing up. Before being traded to Vancouver he won the Memorial Cup with the Windsor Spitfires and a silver medal at the 2011 World Juniors. _____

2) Never drafted, he played his first four seasons with the Regina Pats of the WHL. After being named their captain, MVP and "Most Popular Player," he signed a contract with the Moose and debuted with the Canucks in '05. He scored on his very first shot. Although his career was tragically cut short, he will always be remembered as a fan favourite and an incredible fighter.

_____

3) A 4th-overall selection, his team won back-to-back President's Cups as QMJHL champions, and he holds the QMJHL record for most career playoff games. Turning pro in '99 with the Lowell Lock Monsters, he became an NHL regular in 2000. Before all that, his parents wanted him to pursue a soccer career, but since age 14 he wisely focused on hockey. _____

4) A first-round selection, this Canuck helped his home-state Minnesota Golden Gophers to back-to-back NCAA championships in '02 and '03, amassing 100 points over 123 games. Before playing an NHL game, he had been a member of three NHL teams. He also played for the U.S. at the '04 World Championships, helping his country to a bronze medal. _____

5) This player had a very successful youth career before joining the Canucks. He captured a gold medal at the 2001 World U17 Hockey Challenge, won the Best Player Award at the '02 IIHF World U18 Championships, and helped lead his country to a World Junior Championship in '04 (after being released by the Canucks organization to play). _____

6) Selected 51st overall, this Canuck earned his stripes in the AJHL with the Camrose Kodiaks for two seasons, where he was named league MVP in 2005 and led all scorers with 10 points in five games at the Royal Bank Cup. The next year he headed to the WCHA's University of Minnesota–Duluth, where he recorded 74 points in 79 games over two years. He made his international debut for Canada at the 2010 IIHF World Championships. _____

· · · · · · · · · · · · · · · · · · · ·

*The Canucks finished the 2010 playoffs with a dismal 68.5% penalty kill. In 2011 they finished with 80.8%, and improved to 88.8% in 2012.*

**7)** Selected 53rd-overall in 2004, this American received heavy critisicm over a hunting incident in 2012. Before joining the Canucks he earned his former team's "Player of the Year" award in '09, but two serious concussions have slowed down his production recently.

_____

**8)** Named the Manitoba Moose Rookie of the Year in his only full AHL season, he was selected from a third-tier Swedish "beer league" team (as described by Canucks scouting staff), and played 22 games for the Canucks a mere two years after that draft. _____

**9)** This American was chosen in the first round back in 2002 by Montreal. He began his career by posting three-straight 20 goal seasons, but during his next three seasons he appeared on four different teams. He has since settled in with Vancouver, claiming the Fred J. Hume trophy as the team's "unsung hero" of 2011–12. _____

**10)** This Canuck was the '05 International Ball Hockey Player of the Year, and entered the Canadian Ball Hockey Hall of Fame in '10. Despite never being drafted, he worked his way through the ECHL, eventually establishing himself as an NHLer with a four-year deal in '09. _____

**11)** Before becoming a 3rd-overall pick, he played with Modo of the Swedish Elite League, the same team as his brother and their father before them. At age 16 he recorded 5 points in his first season. For two weeks he was stuck in the minors while his brother played on Modo's senior club, one of the only times they have played on a different team. He improved to 34 points his second year and a team-leading 47 in his final season. He was a co-recipient (along with his brother) of the "Guldpucken" award in '99 for player of the year in Sweden. _____

**12)** After a humble 12 points in his rookie campaign with Modo, this future 2nd-overall draft pick led the team in scoring the next season and finished second to his brother in his final year. His first NHL goal came in his third game, a game-tying goal in the last 90 seconds against Tampa, assisted by his brother. Later that year, after missing a few games with an injury, he was called out by Marc Crawford who said playing with pain is an NHL job requirement. _____

**13)** This BC boy played four years with the WHL's Prince George Cougars. He was WHL Defenseman of the Year and Player of the Year in '02. A mainstay on Canada's World Championship teams since '06, he also played on the '01 and '02 World Junior squads. _____

• • • • • • • • • • • • • • • • • • •

_Wayne Gretzky scored both his first career goal and his record-setting 802nd goal against Vancouver._

# Notable Names

Can you match up all of these notable members of the Canucks organization?

| | |
|---|---|
| Stan Smyl | Public address announcer since '87 |
| Mike Gillis | Current anthem singer |
| Nathan Lafayette | Former anthem singer |
| Mike Burnstein | First-ever draft pick |
| Cyclone Taylor | Equipment manager |
| Mark Donnelly | Head athletic trainer |
| Barry Wilkins | Chief scout |
| Richard Loney | Scored first Canucks goal |
| Ron Delorme | Hit post in Game 7 of '94 Finals |
| Pat O'Neill | First captain |
| Trevor Linden | Almost voted to '07 All-Star Game |
| Andre Boudrias | First Canuck to 100 goals |
| John Ashbridge | First Canuck to 200 goals |
| Francesco Aquilini | First Canuck to 300 goals |
| Orland Kurtenbach | Vancouver Millionaires star |
| Rory Fitzpatrick | General manager |
| Dale Tallon | Owner |

• • • • • • • • • • • • • • • • • • •

*Roberto Luongo has taken three penalties over the last three seasons. Dan Cloutier, meanwhile, averaged 22 penalty minutes from '02 through '04, including 10 more playoff PIMs.*

# P's and Q's

Can you answer all these questions?

1) What is the most common last name in Canuck history?
   A) Smith       B) Brown       C) Johnson

2) Three pairs of brothers have played for Vancouver at the same time. Who are they?
   A) _____
   B) _____
   C) _____

3) Players with last names beginning with every letter except these two have laced up for Vancouver. Which two letters are not represented?
   A) X and Y          C) X and Q
   B) X and U          D) X and Z

4) 60 players with last names beginning with this letter have played for Vancouver, the most of any letter.
   A) S       B) B       C) M

5) Can you name three players from 2011–12 whose first and last names both start with the same letter?
   A) _____
   B) _____
   C) _____

6) Which Canuck player had the longest name?
   A) Vadim Sharifijanov (17 letters)
   B) Sheldon Kannegiesser (19 letters)
   C) Vladimir Konstantinentov (23 letters)

· · · · · · · · · · · · · · · · · · · ·

**Q:** *Watch out, Cory! Which Canuck infamously struck his own goalie in the head with his stick, in an accidental fit of rage?*

# SudoClue #2

Answer the clues below, corresponding to their location in the grid on the facing page. Each clue is answered with a number which then goes into the four locations listed in brackets. This is a sudoku grid, meaning each row, column and 3x3 grid must have the numbers 1–9 in it only once each. After you've filled in the clues, you'll need to complete the grid according to this rule. We've filled in a few numbers to start you off.

1) # of Game 7's Vancouver played in 2011 [A1, D6, E9, H7]

2) # of Stanley Cups won by Vancouver teams [A7, F2, G1, H4]

3) Minimum # of players on the ice (both teams combined) [A4, B9, D1, G3]

4) Hole between Kirk McLean's legs (or any goalie) [C5, E3, F9, G7]

5) # of games between Vancouver and Edmonton in 2012-13 [B5, F6, G2, H8]

6) # the Canucks "retired" in 2008 in honour of their fans [B3, C9, F5, I8]

7) Minimum # of faceoffs in a game [C1, D8, G6, I3]

8) The Canucks finished the season in 199__ with 23 wins, and their lowest winning percentage since 1973 [A8, C6, F1, G9]

9) The Sedins became Canucks in 199__ [B2, D7, E4, H3]

10) The Canucks have never won this many playoff series' in one year [C4, D3, G8, H2]

11) Including Vancouver, the # of teams that joined the NHL in 1970 [C8, F3, G5, I2]

· · · · · · · · · · · · · · · · · ·

*As kids, the Sedins played on Peter Forsberg's backyard hockey rink. They later played their minor hockey with Jarved, the same organization as Markus Naslund.*

|   | 1 | 2 | 3 | 4 | 5 | 6 | 7 | 8 | 9 |
|---|---|---|---|---|---|---|---|---|---|
| A |   |   |   |   |   |   |   |   |   |
| B |   |   |   |   |   |   |   |   |   |
| C |   | 8 |   |   |   |   | 6 |   |   |
| D |   |   |   |   |   |   |   |   | 6 |
| E |   |   |   |   | 4 |   |   |   |   |
| F |   |   |   |   |   |   |   |   |   |
| G |   |   |   |   |   |   |   |   |   |
| H | 7 |   |   |   |   |   |   |   |   |
| I |   |   |   |   | 9 |   |   |   |   |

**Q:** *Who did Alex Burrows accuse in 2010 of having a personal vendetta against him?*

# Line Change

Can you pick the year that all three players were Canuck teammates?

**1)** Mathieu Schneider, Steve Bernier, Mason Raymond
- A) 2009–10
- B) 2008–09
- C) 2007–08
- D) 2006–07

**2)** Gino Odjick, Alex Mogilny, Garth Snow
- A) 1992–93
- B) 1995–96
- C) 1997–98
- D) 2000–01

**3)** Trevor Linden, Matt Cooke, Luc Bourdon
- A) 2006–07
- B) 2007–08
- C) 2008–09
- D) 2009–10

**4)** Taylor Pyatt, Jan Bulis, Jeff Cowan
- A) 2005–06
- B) 2006–07
- C) 2007–08
- D) 2008–09

**5)** Darcy Rota, Ivan Boldirev, Colin Campbell
- A) 1973–74
- B) 1977–78
- C) 1981–82
- D) 1987–88

**6)** Rick Rypien, Jarkko Ruutu, Wade Brookbank
- A) 2001–02
- B) 2003–04
- C) 2004–05
- D) 2005–06

• • • • • • • • • • • • • • • • • •

*Over his six-year NHL career, Martin Brochu briefly played for the Canucks, Caps and Pens. The unlucky netminder made nine starts and lost every game.*

# Fill Me In

Can you answer all of these questions?  We've filled in some letters to help you out.

**1)** Name all the main Sedin linemates during their career

2000–01: __ R _ _ _ _    _ _ L _ _ _ _    &    _ _ D _ _    _ E _ _ U _ _ _ _

2001–02: _ _ _ E _ _ _    _ _ _ A _ _ _

2002–03: T _ _ _ _ _    _ _ _ _ _ T   &   _ R _ _ _ _ _    L _ _ _ _ _ N

2003–04: J _ _ _ _ _ _    _ _ _ G &   _ _ G _ _ _ _    A _ _ _ _ _ S _ _

2005–06: _ N _ _ _ _    C _ _ _ _ _ _

2006–07: _ A _ _ _ _ _    _ _ A _ _ _

2007–08: _ _ _ Y _ _ _ _    _ Y _ _ _ _   & M _ _ _ _ _ S    _ _ _ _ _ _ _ D

2008–09: _ _ E _    _ _ _ R _ _ _ _   &   _ _ V _ _    _ E _ _ _ R _

        &    _ _ _ _ _ E    _ _ _ _ N I _ _ _

2009–10 and 2010–11: _ _ _ _ _    _ _ U _ _ _ _ _ _   &

                    _ _ _ _ _ E _    _ A _ _ _ _ _ _ _ _

**2)** Name Luongo's backups:

2006–07: D _ _ _ _    _ _ _ _ _ U _ _ _ _

2007–08: _ U _ _ _ _ _    _ _ _ _ _ _ _ D

2008–09: _ _ R _ _ _ _    _ _ N _ _ _ _ _   &   _ _ _ _ _ N L _ _ _ _ _ _ _ _ _

2009–10: _ _ _ _ _ _ _ _    _ _ _ C _ _ _ _ _

2010–12: _ _ _ _ _    _ _ _ _ _ _ _ _ _ _

**3)** Since the lockout the Nucks have played 40 games against each of these four teams

_ _ _ G _ _ _ _ ,    _ _ _ _ _ _ _ _ _ O ,

_ _ _ O _ _ _ _ _   &   _ _ _ _ _ _ _ O _ _

**4)** Canucks four highest paid players in 2011–12 (going by overall cap hit, not salary)

#1: _ _ _ _ _ _ _ _    _ _ _ _ _ N      #3: _ _ _ _ E _ _ _ _    _ _ _ _ _ _ _ _

#2: _ _ _ _ _ I _    _ _ _ _ _ _      #4: _ _ _ _ _    _ _ _ L _ _

• • • • • • • • • • • • • • • • • • •

*Bill LaForge has the lowest points of any Canuck coach, registering just 10 points before getting fired 20 games into the '84 season.*

# True or False

Can you decipher fact from fiction?

1) In Canuck history, only nine players have worn a jersey number higher than 58.

        **True**                     **False**

2) The Canucks have never had more than two head coaches during one season.

        **True**                     **False**

3) The Canucks have only had one non-Canadian captain.

        **True**                     **False**

4) The Canucks only played three road games in the 2012 Playoffs.

        **True**                     **False**

5) Of the 12 best Canuck seasons (going by most points in regular season), ten of them have happened since 2000.

        **True**                     **False**

6) In his four career games against Vancouver, Pavel Bure did not record a single point.

        **True**                     **False**

7) Markus Naslund, Peter Forsberg and the Sedins all played together for Modo in Sweden at the same time.

        **True**                     **False**

8) Since entering the league, Henrik Sedin has only missed 10 games.

        **True**                     **False**

• • • • • • • • • • • • • • • • • •

*The 1998–99 Canucks had 717 more penalty minutes than the 1999–00 team (1,764 to 1,047).*

**9)** Markus Naslund has the 17th-most penalty minutes in Canuck history.

                    **True**                    **False**

**10)** In 2005–06, Alex Auld won the team's Cyclone Taylor Award for MVP.

                    **True**                    **False**

**11)** From 1999 to 2010, only two players have led the Canucks in total points in the regular season.

                    **True**                    **False**

**12)** Trevor Linden never led the team in points for a single-season campaign.

                    **True**                    **False**

**13)** Daniel Sedin (+36), Christian Ehrhoff (+36) and Henrik Sedin (+35) occupy/share the #1, #2 and #3 spots in best single-season Canuck plus/minus records. All three did it in 2009–10.

                    **True**                    **False**

**14)** Going by penalty minutes per game, the Canucks are the fifth-most penalized team in NHL history, trailing only Buffalo, Philadelphia, Boston and Pittsburgh.

                    **True**                    **False**

**15)** Dan Cloutier holds the single-season record for lowest GAA as a Canuck.

                    **True**                    **False**

**16)** Donald Brashear led the NHL in fighting majors for two straight years ('97–'98), only the second time in history a player has done so (Rob Ray also did it in the 90s).

                    **True**                    **False**

• • • • • • • • • • • • • • • • • • •

**Q:** *Which Canuck won the NHL Foundation Player Award in 2008, for dedication and commitment to the community?*

# Road Trip

In 2010, the Canucks battled through the longest road trip in NHL history. Can you answer all the questions, picking the correct numbers from the box below? Cross out each number as you go.

1) # of days _____

2) # of games _____

3) # of cities _____

4) # of kilometres travelled between games _____

5) # of wins _____

6) # of losses _____

7) # of OT/SO losses _____

8) # of weeks' break during the trip for the Olympic Games _____

9) # of times team played back-to-back games _____

10) # of hours spent travelling on planes between games _____

11) # of games in final 9 days of trip _____

12) # of people in attendance in Chicago (highest) _____

13) # of people in attendance in Colorado (lowest) _____

14) # of goals scored _____

15) # of goals allowed _____

16) # of games at home out of the last 15 after the trip _____

17) # of sticks brought by the team _____

18) # of games both Calgary & Philly played on the road (old record) _____

| | | | | |
|---|---|---|---|---|
| 1 | 6 | 13 | 45 | |
| 2 | 8 | 14 | 47 | 20,737 |
| 3 | 10 | 30 | 300 | 22,235 |
| 5 | 11 | 42 | 12,861 | |

**Q:** *Can you name Vancouver's 2012 playoff leader in these categories?*
*1) points  2) average ice time  3) penalty minutes  4) plus/minus  5) faceoff %  6) GWG*

# Goalie Graveyard

In between Roberto Luongo and Kirk McLean, 15 goalies suited up for more than 100 minutes for Vancouver. Can you unscramble all of them?

1) Leifx Vintop _____

2) Rahgt Nows _____

3) Rocey Bwasch _____

4) Vinek Eweske _____

5) Oycer Rihhsc _____

6) Sturar Bire _____

7) Lexa Dalu _____

8) And Crutolie _____

9) Mamexi Toleule _____

10) Maik Roonnen _____

11) Nojah Grehdbe _____

12) Peert Drukas _____

13) Timarn Bourch _____

14) Obb Snasese _____

15) Neas Rubke _____

• • • • • • • • • • • • • • •

**Q:** *Who were the members of these five Canuck lines?*
*1) Mattress Line  2) Ikea Line  3) Westcoast Express  4) The Brothers Line  5) The Life Line*

# The Trade

The Canucks have been shaped (and mis-shaped) by many trades over the years. See if you can fill in the missing information for all of the key trades below. To help you out, all the missing information is in the box on the facing page. Cross out each as you go.

| Canucks Got | From | Canucks Gave | Year |
|---|---|---|---|
| 1) Markus Naslund | _____ | _____ | 1996 |
| 2) Barry Pedersen | _____ | _____ | 1986 |
| 3) _____ _____ _____ | _____ | Trevor Linden | 1998 |
| 4) _____ _____ | San Jose | Patrick White, Daniel Rahimi | 2009 |
| 5) Matt Pettinger | Washington | _____ | 2008 |
| 6) _____ _____ _____ | _____ | Bryan Allen, Alex Auld, Todd Bertuzzi | 2006 |
| 7) Robert Dirk, 5th-round pick ('92), _____ _____ _____ | St. Louis | Garth Butcher, Dan Quinn | 1991 |
| 8) Brendan Morrison, Denis Pedersen | _____ | _____ | 2000 |

. . . . . . . . . . . . . . . . . . . .

*The 1986–87 season set the franchise record low of 10,406 average fans per game.*

| Canucks Got | From | Canucks Gave | Year |
|---|---|---|---|
| **9)** Sami Salo | _____ | _____ | 2002 |
| **10)** 5th-round pick ('81), _____ | NY Islanders | 5th-round pick ('81) | 1980 |
| **11)** _____ _____ _____ _____ _____ | Florida | Bret Hedican, Brad Ference, Cond. 3rd-round pick, _____ | 1999 |
| **12)** _____ | Florida | Evan Oberg, _____ | 2011 |
| **13)** _____ _____ | Florida | Steve Bernier, _____ _____ | 2010 |
| **14)** 2nd-round pick ('07), Conditional pick ('09) | Los Angeles | _____ | 2006 |
| **15)** Trevor Linden, 2nd-round pick ('09) | _____ | 1st-round pick ('02), 3rd-round pick ('03) | 2001 |

| | | | | |
|---|---|---|---|---|
| **Ottawa** | **Alek Stojanov** | **Michael Grabner** | **Alexander Mogilny** | **Chris Higgins** |
| **Boston** | **Keith Ballard** | **Dan Cloutier** | **Victor Oreskovich** | **3rd-round pick ('98)** |
| **Florida** | **Ed Jovanovski** | **Brad Lukowich** | **Pavel Bure** | **6th-round pick ('06)** |
| **Washington** | **Cam Neely** | **Sergio Momesso** | **Kevin Weekes** | **1st-round pick ('10)** |
| **New Jersey** | **Todd Bertuzzi** | **Bryan McCabe** | **Mike Brown** | **3rd-round pick ('13)** |
| **Pittsburgh** | **Dave Gagner** | **Lukas Krajicek** | **Matt Cooke** | **Cond. 1st-round pick** |
| **NY Islanders** | **Roberto Luongo** | **Geoff Courtnall** | **Christian Ehrhoff** | |
| | **Cliff Ronning** | **Peter Schaefer** | **Richard Brodeur** | |

• • • • • • • • • • • • • •

*In winning the Hart as league MVP, Henrik Sedin finished with six more first-place votes than Ovechkin, and 26 more than Crosby. In 2011, Daniel trailed Hart-winner Corey Perry by 16 first-place votes.*

# Faceoff

## Across
1) Canuck power forward traded to Boston, where he is now team president
4) Six Canucks in 2012–13 are this nationality
6) Cup parade would be planned down this street
11) AKA jääkiekko in Finnish
12) In 1986, this Swede was the franchise's all-time scoring leader (first name)
14) Four-time Nucks' "hardest shot" winner (last name)
15) The Canucks had 48 of these in 1994–95
17) Seen on the boards
18) First name of Canuck who served longest suspension in club history
19) Robitaille, Keane, Brown
21) Tanner Glass, Martin Gelinas and Donald Brashear all played here
24) You don't want too many of these on the ice
26) 1994, 2005–06
28) Markus Naslund and Ilya Kovalchuk chased a puck out of the arena and through the city in an ad for this company
29) Former Canucks affiliate from Victoria (two words)

## Down
1) Home division
2) Ryan Kesler underwent surgery on this body part in the summer of 2011
3) First name of Canucks GM, coach and president during 1993
5) Former D-man who suffered an eye injury in his 3rd season (first name)
7) This kind of goalie didn't play much for Vancouver after 2006
8) Lou missed the start of this during an '09 bathroom break
9) Former D-man's nickname, minus "cop"
10) Former GM of Canucks (first name)
13) Type of Canuck rocket
14) Tambellini, Staios, Weeks
16) Last name of Nucks PIM leader, with 459 more PIMs than anyone else
19) General _____
20) You can't score a goal if you did this to the puck
21) Rogers Arena chant
22) Last name of Canuck named Most Exciting Player from '84 through '88
23) Bud Poile was the first one of these
25) Players can lose this while on the ice
27) Number of Canucks with 30 or more points in 2011–12

• • • • • • • • • • • • • • • • • • • •

*The Canucks jerseys have underwent six distinct changes. Trevor Linden has worn four of them.*

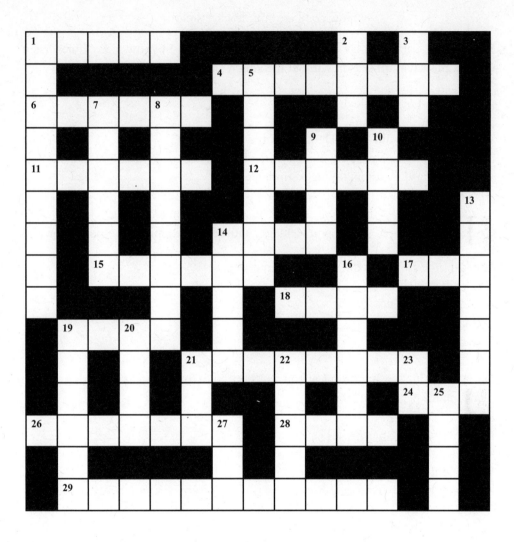

*Christian Ehrhoff's 50 points in 2010–11 are the most ever by a German d-man, passing Uwe Krupp's old record of 44 (which Ehrhoff tied in 2009–10).*

# More Choice

How good are your hockey smarts?

1) Since the 82-game regular season was adopted in 1995–96, how many times has a Canuck played a full season without missing a single game?
A) 9          C) 58
B) 29         D) 79

2) What strange stat did Pavol Demitra record in 2009–10?
A) He did not take a penalty, the only time a Canuck has played more than 25 games in one season without taking a single penalty.
B) He scored 80% of his goals when the opposition goalie was pulled (he only scored five goals in the year, four of them into the empty net).
C) He led the team in shooting percentage, with 52.9%, despite only scoring nine goals.

3) The last time Henrik Sedin missed a game was...
A) October, 2009
B) February, 2007
C) March, 2004
D) November, 2001

4) During his nine seasons with Vancouver, Sami Salo missed an average of how many games per season?
A) 9          C) 34
B) 19         D) 42

5) Which of these Sedin facts is not true?
A) At age 15, both were members of the Swedish National Junior soccer team.
B) In 2010 they donated $1.5 million to help build a new BC Children's Hospital.
C) Daniel's first-ever international goal came in the '98 World Championships against Canada – a breakaway goal on Roberto Luongo.
D) According to their father, they did not begin playing organized ice hockey until age 10.

• • • • • • • • • • • • • • • • • • • • •

*In 2009–10, the average number of TV viewers who tuned in for Toronto, Montreal, Vancouver and Calgary games combined was more than all 24 US teams combined. The Canucks viewership alone eclipsed the 11 least-watched teams in the league, combined.*

**6)** Which of these unorthodox moves did Mike Gillis NOT make?
A) Built a "MindRoom" for the team. Straight out of a sci-fi novel, players in this room have electrodes attached to their body while they enter a relaxed, meditative state. This calmness will hopefully be channelled during games.
B) In order to gauge sleep patterns and identify fatigue levels, players in 2008 wore "biorhythm bracelets" that monitored their inner circadian rhythms.
C) Strict targets for weight and body-fat percentage are enforced. Working under an executive chef, many players have been put on specific meal plans, having every meal of the day specially prepared.
D) A travelling spa follows the team, featuring nine masseuses, four acupuncturists, a traditional Native American healer and even an aesthetician (for pedicures).

**7)** How many V's were on the Canucks infamous "flying V" jerseys?
A) 1      C) 7
B) 3      D) 11

**8)** Where did Bobby Lou wear his captaincy "C"?
A) On his mask
B) On his jersey
C) He wasn't allowed to visibly display the "C" because of his position
D) On the blade of his stick

**9)** In 1977, the NHL required that all jerseys have player names printed on the back. What were the first words to appear on the front of Canuck jerseys?
A) Vancouver
B) Canucks
C) Original
D) NHL

**10)** Of the 32 Canucks who played at least one game in the 1970–71 season, how many were still in the NHL five years later?
A) 3        C) 16
B) 9        D) 24

• • • • • • • • • • • • • • • • • • •

**Q:** *The longest Canuck winning streak (2002) and the longest losing streak (1997) are the same number of games. How many?  A) 8  B) 10  C) 12  D) 14*

# Word Work

How many words can you make from the letters in "Vancouver" and "Canucks"? Each letter can only be used once per word, no proper names are allowed, and the words must be at least three letters long (like Boggle). Pluralizing a word does not count it twice. We found 67 in Vancouver and 16 in Canucks, how many can you find?

## VANCOUVER

_____  _____
_____  _____
_____  _____
_____  _____
_____  _____
_____  _____
_____  _____
_____  _____
_____  _____
_____  _____
_____  _____
_____  _____
_____  _____
_____  _____

## CANUCKS

_____
_____
_____
_____
_____
_____
_____
_____
_____
_____
_____
_____
_____
_____

• • • • • • • • • • • • • • • • •

**Q:** *True or False: In 2011–12, Mason Raymond and Ryan Kesler combined for 14 shootout attempts. Together, they scored three times.*

# Spot the Fakes

Each of the lists below has two made-up names. Can you spot all the fakes?

### 1) Player Names

Mario Marios
Jiri Bubla
Lubomir Vaic
Steven Pen
Cesare Maniago
Lonny Bohonos
Leif Rohlin
Evgeny Namestnikov
Red Brown
Paul Lawless

### 3) Canuck Birthplaces

Moers
Most
Brno
St. Malo
Maniwaki
Gorky
The Corner
Karlovy Vary
Bagel
South Porcupine

### 2) Player Names

Anatoli Semenov
Stu Kulak
Darryl Sly
Ron Homenuke
Mike Lampman
Ab T. Demarco
Bob Manno
Per-Olov Brasar
Randy Quick
Radulan Hrzck

### 4) Canuck Birthplaces

Myjava
Itzehoe
Ufa
Bakkenfraz
Storatuna
Warman
Bend
Lose
Viking
Murmansk

• • • • • • • • • • • • • • • • • •

**Q:** *Only two coaches in Canuck history coached the team for more than three complete seasons. Can you name them both?*

# Playoff Puzzle

Can you answer all of these questions about the Canucks 2011 playoffs?

1) Which Canuck(s) received a suspension during the 2011 playoffs?
   A) Alex Burrows (1 game) and Aaron Rome (4 games).
   B) Aaron Rome (2 games) and Raffi Torres (2 games).
   C) Alex Burrows (1 game) and Raffi Torres (1 game).
   D) Aaron Rome (4 games).

2) Which of these facts about Ryan Kesler is true?
   A) Of the 14 goals Vancouver scored against Nashville, Kesler either scored or assisted 11 of them.
   B) Kesler scored all of Vancouver's game-winning goals against Nashville.
   C) Before this season, Kesler had not scored a single goal in the playoffs.
   D) All of the above.

3) Against Chicago, the Canucks almost became the next team to give up a 3–0 lead and lose a series. How many NHL teams have accomplished this unfortunate feat? Bonus: Can you name those team(s)?
   A) 1
   B) 3
   C) 7
   D) 11

4) What playoff record did the Canucks set in a game against San Jose?
   A) The Canucks became the first (and only) team to win a playoff game without winning a single faceoff in the third period.
   B) Most 5-on-3 goals in one game (the Canucks had three).
   C) Most blocked shots by one team in one game (the Canucks blocked 31, including an impressive 15 in the third period).
   D) Fewest shots allowed by one team in one game (Canucks allowed 9).

• • • • • • • • • • • • • • • • • • •

*Over the past four seasons, the Sedins have 707 points in 627 regular-season games, good for 1.13 ppg. In the playoffs, they have 97 points in 99 games.*

**5)** A May 31, 2011 poll by Ipsos-Reid/Rogers Sportsnet found that what percentage of Canadians were cheering for Vancouver to win the Cup?
A) 35%
B) 49%
C) 62%
D) 74%

**6)** Sami Salo was the oldest member of the 2011 Canucks by roughly two years. After him, who were the next three oldest Vancouver players, in order?
A) Roberto Luongo, Chris Higgins, Manny Malhotra
B) Chris Higgins, Mikael Samuelsson, Manny Malhotra
C) Raffi Torres, Chris Higgins, Roberto Luongo
D) Mikael Samuelsson, Roberto Luongo, Manny Malhotra

**7)** Which of these things did Roberto Luongo NOT say during the Stanley Cup Finals against Boston?
A) (On the winning goal from Game 1), "It's an easy save for me, but if you're wondering out and aggressive like he (Thomas) does, that's going to happen. He might make some saves that I won't."
B) (On Thomas), "I have been pumping his tires ever since the series started. I haven't heard one nice thing he had to say about me. That's the way it is."
C) (On Burrows supposedly biting a finger), "Look, if you had someone's stinky gloves in your mouth, and they hadn't washed them all year, you would do the same thing."

**8)** Which of these stat-facts are NOT true?
A) Only ten Canucks played in every playoff game.
B) Only six Canuck skaters finished with a positive plus/minus.
C) Cory Schneider appeared in five games, totalling 163 minutes of action.
D) No Canuck players finished in the top five for overall playoff points.

• • • • • • • • • • • • • • • • • •

**Q:** *How many times has former Canucks broadcaster Jim Hughson called the Stanley Cup Finals for CBC?* *A) 1* *B) 2* *C) 3* *D) 4*

# Top 20 Search

The last names of the top 20 all-time point leaders in Canuck history are hidden below.
As a bonus, can you fill in all their first names?

| S | U | N | D | S | T | R | O | M | M | O | T | B |
|---|---|---|---|---|---|---|---|---|---|---|---|---|
| N | A | S | I | L | S | N | L | I | O | O | G | E |
| S | E | I | U | I | E | I | Y | Y | G | N | G | R |
| I | E | M | R | N | D | D | M | D | I | L | S | T |
| O | M | D | L | D | A | E | S | N | L | Y | K | R |
| E | H | Y | I | E | U | S | N | K | N | Y | R | E |
| L | U | L | B | N | V | O | L | V | Y | G | I | L |
| I | Z | Z | U | T | R | E | B | U | R | R | K | S |
| T | A | N | R | N | V | U | R | Z | N | A | O | E |
| N | A | S | E | E | D | Z | S | M | A | D | A | K |
| A | K | E | A | R | N | S | Z | Z | U | I | N | S |
| T | K | N | O | S | I | R | R | O | M | N | Z | I |

ADAMS     LEVER     SEDIN
BERTUZZI     LINDEN     SEDIN
BOUDRIAS     LUMME     SKRIKO
BURE     MORRISON     SMYL
GRADIN     NASLUND     SUNDSTROM
KEARNS     OHLUND     TANTI
KESLER     RONNING

**Q:** *Can you rank the players above from 1st to 20th, based on standings through 2011–12?*

# Canuck Killers

Over the years, many players have emerged as true Canuck killers – otherwise good players who perform extraordinarily on the West Coast. Maybe it's the rainy weather, the scenic views, or the suspect quality of hockey played here at times. Can you fill in the missing first or last names of these 15 players, listed beside their career stats against Vancouver?

1) Joe _____    This BC native has 96 pts in 77 games

2) _____    A ridiculous 239 pts in 117 games, a career high

3) Milan _____    A career-best 65 pts in 72 games

4) Andrew _____    59 points in 70 games, 13 more points against Canucks than any other team

5) Adam _____    Career-best 26 pts in 37 games, but suffered a career-altering concussion fighting Ed Jovanovski

6) _____    This Finn has 79 pts in 68 games, maybe a reason why Mike Peca levelled him open-ice in 1995

7) Curtis _____    Future Canuck backup was 5-0-0-2, 1.56 GAA

8) Marty _____    This goalie is 18-7-0-2, 1.92 GAA

9) _____ Walz    Not normally a scorer, he has 20 pts in 44 games, and 10 pts in seven playoff games

10) Kristian _____    28 pts in 35 games

11) Peter _____    57 pts in 44 games

12) _____ Stoll    25 pts in 42 games, plus two playoff goals

13) Theo _____    72 pts in 68 games

14) _____ Backman    D-man has 9% of his points against Vancouver

15) Mark _____    1.52 pts/game against Van, 0.78 pts/game with Van

• • • • • • • • • • • • • • •

*Markus Naslund's 630 points in the 2000s was the 8th-most of the decade; Joe Thornton held the crown with 806 points. Other notables are Mats Sundin at #13 (624), Pavol Demitra at #28 (545) and Todd Bertuzzi at #34 (516).*

# Quotables

Can you pick the correct quote and answer all these questions?

1) AV, asked by a reporter before Game 4 vs LA if the Canucks deserved a break:
   A) "We deserve forty years worth of breaks."
   B) "Breaks? Cars need brakes. Kit Kat bars have breaks. Hockey teams need to win games."
   C) "The hockey gods are a fickle bunch. This season we brought in an Indian guru to meditate on our behalf during each game. We're going to fire him."

2) Canucks GM Brian Burke commenting on the Sedins after a 2002 playoff game against the Detroit Red Wings:
   A) "'Sedin' is not Swedish for 'punch me or headlock me in a scrum.'"
   B) "The sisters really need to step it up next game."
   C) "Apparently [Detroit] really like twins, they couldn't keep their hands off them all night."

3) Who did Mikael Samuelsson tell to "Go _____ themselves"?
   A) The Red Wings, after they offered him a $600,000 pay cut for a 2008 contract.
   B) The Swedish Olympic selection committee, after they didn't select him.
   C) The Chicago Blackhawks, after Dustin Byfuglien taunted Vancouver fans after scoring a playoff goal.

4) After winning the Hart Trophy, Henrik said:
   A) "Daniel...There's no way you can tell me you're the better player right now."
   B) "First of all, I want to thank my family and friends and..." he pauses and walks off the stage laughing, as the real Henrik walks up to the stage. Daniel had pretended to accept the award!
   C) "I want to dedicate this to every twin out there who thinks they'll never be different from their brother. Where's your trophy, Daniel?"

• • • • • • • • • • • • • • • • • • • • • • • • •

*Stan Smyl, on opening night of the flying-V sweaters: "I've never been ashamed to wear the Canucks uniform, but that night none of us wanted to leave the dressing room."*

**5)** Who said this? "I'm not happy with the hit I took. I'm disappointed in the league. I'm disappointed in Colin Campbell. Disappointed that he didn't rule down anything on the play. That's his job. As we've seen, he's been very inconsistent."
A) Alex Burrows
B) Steve Moore
C) Willie Mitchell

**6)** Who said this? "Pat [Quinn] was like a father to me. ... He taught me not only about the game, but how to be a professional and treat people with respect. When I heard his voice and what he had to say, it meant a lot."
A) Trevor Linden
B) Kirk McLean
C) Gino Odjick

**7)** After reporters tried to find out what injury Sami Salo had suffered, he coyly said:
A) "I took a 100-mile-an-hour slapshot to the Sami's."
B) "Maybe it's just a burning sensation when you pee. You never know."
C) "I never have injury problems, so this is a new situation."

**8)** "We compete at everything," Daniel Sedin once said. "No, not everything," interjected Henrik, who added:
A) "We have different girlfriends. I like mine and not his."
B) "Daniel is very good at washing dishes. I encourage him to do the cleaning a lot."
C) "I beat Daniel so bad at Scrabble on the last road trip that he refused to play me ever again. He got something like 78 points over the whole game."

**9)** Ryan Kesler, speaking during the Olympics about Team Canada:
A) "The gold medal game is bigger than the NHL, the Stanley Cup... it's bigger than hockey; this is going to be war."
B) "Well, it's going to be a huge game for us, obviously. With Luongo in net we know they'll give up at least one easy goal. We've got to take advantage of that."
C) "I hate them."

• • • • • • • • • • • • • • • • • • • • • •

*In 74 shootouts, the Canucks are 34–40, good for a 23rd-best. They have scored 85 goals on 256 attempts, and allowed 97 goals on 263 attempts.*

# SudoClue #3

Answer the clues below, corresponding to their locations in the grid on the following page. Each clue is answered with a jersey #, and that number goes into the four locations listed in brackets. If a player's # is "16," his "first #" is 1 and his "second #" is 6. This is a sudoku grid, meaning each row, column and 3x3 grid must have the numbers 1–9 in it only once each. After you've filled in the clues, you'll need to complete the grid according to this rule. We've filled in a few numbers to start you off.

**1)** One of Todd Bertuzzi's old #'s   [B3, F2, H7, I5]

**2)** One of Daniel Sedin's #'s   [B4, C7, D5, H1]

**3)** One of Henrik Sedin's #'s   [B1, C5, F4, H9]

**4)** Adrian Aucoin & Sami Salo's # with Vancouver   [A7, D8, E3, I1]

**5)** Chris Tanev's # and Willie Mitchell's # with Vancouver   [C1, D3, G5, I7]

**6)** Alex Burrows & Ryan Kesler's first #   [E7, F1, H5, I9]

**7)** One of Ed Jovanovski's #'s   [A4, B8, F9, I2]

**8)** Mikael Samuelsson & Jannik Hansen's second #   [B2, F5, G9, H4]

**9)** Brendan Morrison & Cliff Ronning's # with Vancouver   [C9, D2, E6, F7]

**10)** Marco Sturm and Cory Schneider's second #   [C3, D1, G7, H6]

**11)** Pavel Bure's first # (from his first jersey, worn '95 through '97)   [A5, D9, G4, I3]

**12)** Kevin Bieksa & Bret Hedican's #   [A8, D7, G3, I6]

• • • • • • • • • • • • • • • • • •

*Forbes.com values the 2012 Canucks at $300 mil, seventh-highest in the league. Toronto tops the list at $521 mil. The Rangers are second with $507 mil, then Montreal at $445 mil, Detroit at $336 mil, Boston at $325 mil, and Chicago at $306 mil.*

|   | 1 | 2 | 3 | 4 | 5 | 6 | 7 | 8 | 9 |
|---|---|---|---|---|---|---|---|---|---|
| A |   |   |   |   |   |   |   |   | 4 |
| B |   |   |   |   |   | 1 |   |   |   |
| C |   |   |   |   |   |   |   |   |   |
| D |   |   |   |   |   |   |   |   |   |
| E |   |   |   |   | 5 |   |   |   |   |
| F |   |   |   |   |   |   |   | 8 |   |
| G |   |   |   |   |   |   |   |   |   |
| H |   |   | 7 |   |   |   |   |   |   |
| I |   |   |   |   |   |   |   |   |   |

*The 2011–12 Canucks travelled 75,359 km, ninth most of any team (LA "won'"with 89,465 km).*
*Guess that whole travel-thing is a little overblown.*

# Line Change #2

Can you pick the year that all three players were Canuck teammates?

**1)** Peter Schaefer, Roberto Luongo, Jeff Tambellini
    A) 2005–06        C) 2009–10
    B) 2008–09        D) 2010–11

**2)** Jyrki Lumme, Peter Zezel, Dave Babych
    A) 1995–96        C) 1997–98
    B) 1996–97        D) 2000–01

**3)** Steve Kariya, Andrew Cassels, Harold Druken
    A) 2001–02        C) 2004–05
    B) 2003–04        D) 2005–06

**4)** Barry Wilkins, Dunc Wilson, Bobby Schmautz
    A) 1970–71        C) 1977–78
    B) 1973–74        D) 1980–81

**5)** Shane O'Brien, Rob Davison, Jannik Hansen
    A) 2006–07        C) 2008–09
    B) 2007–08        D) 2009–10

**6)** Sergio Momesso, Russ Courtnall, Martin Gelinas
    A) 1989–90        C) 1994–95
    B) 1992–93        D) 1997–98

• • • • • • • • • • • • • • • • • •

**Q:** *True or False: In 2012, the Canucks became only the second team since 1990 to win back-to-back President's Trophies. The Wings did it twice; in 1994–95 and 1995–96, and again in 2003–04 and 2005–06.*

# '70s, '80s, '90s or '00s #2

Do you know if each event happened in the 1970s, 1980s, 1990s or 2000s?
If you want more of a challenge, try to guess the exact year.

1) Pavel Bure plays his first game. _____

2) Pavel Bure plays his last game in the NHL. _____

3) Canucks make playoffs for the first time. _____

4) Canucks win first playoff series. _____

5) A Canuck scores 50 goals in a season. (Bonus – who was he?) _____

6) Streak of 15-straight seasons with a losing record finally comes to an end. _____

7) Trevor Linden is drafted with the 2nd-overall pick. _____

8) Stan Smyl retires as the team leader in points (673), goals (262), assists (411)
   and games played (896). _____

9) Igor Larionov plays his first game, en route to a 44-point rookie campaign. _____

10) Cody Hodgson is born. _____

11) Canucks set a franchise record with 105 points and 49 wins. _____

12) A Canuck wins the Lester. B. Pearson award for MVP, as voted by the players.
    (Bonus – who won the award?) _____

13) Canuck players are first seen in yellow, orange, and lots of V's. _____

14) The orange home jerseys are replaced with a more standard white jersey, featuring
    the "Canucks" skate crest. _____

15) The Orca makes its first appearance on Canuck jerseys, and orange is completely
    abandoned. _____

• • • • • • • • • • • • • • • • • •

*Top five total plus/minus in Canucks history: 1. Henrik Sedin (+181), 2. Daniel Sedin (+160),
3. Alex Burrows (+116), 4. Dana Murzyn (+78), 4. Sami Salo (+79). Only 112 players
in Canuck history have a plus/minus above 0 (minimum 10 games played).*

# Ever a Canuck?

Each of these groups of three NHLers has one who never played a regular season or playoff game with the Canucks. Can you circle all of the odd ones out?

1) Gerry O'Flaherty     Petri Skriko     Curt Giles

2) Mika Noronen     Maxime Ouellet     Lorne "Gump" Worsley

3) Evan Oberg     Drew MacIntyre     John Vanbiesbrouck

4) Fedor Fedorov     Owen Nolan     Sergei Shirokov

5) Mathieu Schneider     Mike Sillinger     Steve Sullivan

6) Brad Ference     Tyler Bouck     Michael Grabner

7) Josh Holden     Josh Green     Lee Stempniak

8) Esa Tikkanen     Pat Quinn     Roger Neilson

9) Ian White     Mike Robitaille     Richard Lemieux

10) Manny Legace     Brandon Reid     Curt Fraser

11) Guillaume Desbiens     Steve Begin     Lawrence Nycholat

12) Joel Perrault     Patrick Coulombe     Valeri Bure

**Q:** *Which tough guy holds the Canuck record for most PIMs in a single season, with 372?*

# Up the Middle

Each of these random rows of letters is hiding the full name of a Canuck defenceman, past or present. Fill in the one missing letter in the centre to reveal each name.

1) E L C H R I S A ___ I S A L O N E R

2) T O D D A N H A ___ H U I S E L T H

3) M A T O M A T T ___ A S O H L U N D

4) S B O B R A D O ___ G L I D S T E R

5) L U K A S K R A ___ I C E K I C E K

6) M I K E L R O B ___ E N T S O P E L

7) R O B R Y A N A ___ L E N D O L E S

8) A C H R I S T A ___ E V E R T I N G

9) T R I C K E I T ___ B A L L A R D S

10) D A V E B A B Y ___ H A N D L E R C

11) S W I L L I E M ___ T C H E L L E Y

12) V A N D A N A M ___ R E K M A L I K

13) A L B O B R Y A ___ M C C A B E N G

14) R O B R E T H E ___ I C A N E Y C H

15) J A S O N G A R ___ I S O N R O M E

16) R A H I M A D A ___ A M U R Z Y N G

17) A N D R E W A L ___ E R T S E N D E

· · · · · · · · · · · · · · · · · · · · · · · ·

*A different era: 51 times the 1987–88 Canucks or their opponents registered five or more goals in one game, compared with a mere 13 times in 2007–08. Additionally, 18 times seven or more goals were scored in 1987–88, compared with only twice in 2007–08.*

# In the Crease

**Across**
1) A Canuck won this for the first time in 2010
3) Sedin _____
7) _____ Pyatt
9) In 2009, the Canucks did this for the first time in the modern playoff era
11) Lou struggled in 2010 with pucks deflecting off this part of his stick
13) Last name of the coach who originated 2 Down
16) Rich, one of six brothers in this NHL family, played for Vancouver
18) Smolinski, Allen, McSheffrey
19) First name of NHL's all-time penalty minute leader (a former Canuck)
20) _____ Fitzpatrick
22) The longest one of these Vancouver went on in 2011–12 lasted five games
24) See 21 down (same answer)
25) Canucks beat San Jose in the third _____ in 2011
27) Home rink used to be known as the _____
30) First name of enforcer who succeeded Gino
32) All-time Nucks point leader among defencemen (last name)
33) Something that can be chipped, and a 2009–10 Canuck
34) Some of the Canucks biggest trades in recent history involved this team

**Down**
2) _____ Power
3) This can't happen in the NHL anymore
4) Full name of Canuck who sits second to Linden in games played, with 896
5) _____ Star
6) May, Isbister, Gassoff
8) Patrik _____
10) Place where many lucky Canadians play hockey
12) First name of Canucks' iron-man streak holder (most consecutive games)
14) Type of squad games that happen at training camp
15) First name of Russian with 139 goals and 308 points in 312 games for Vancouver
17) Trevor Linden did this exactly 20 years to the day after being drafted.
21) This gets longer in the second season
23) _____ season
26) Deadline _____
28) Line, judge, scorer
29) Vancouver had seven of these goals in 2010–11
30) _____ - up (aka fisticuffs)
32) _____ season
33) __ __ A (abbreviated goalie stat)

* * * * * * * * * * * * * * * * * * * *

*Trevor Linden's 1,140 games for Vancouver is 244 more games than anyone else. To put this in perspective, only 71 Canuck players have ever played 244 games with the club.*

**Q:** *In an '07 episode of* How I Met Your Mother, *a character says she got into the locker room and met this Canuck player after a game. Neil Patrick Harris' character responds to this with a sarcastic, "What's the opposite of name-dropping?" Who was the player in question?*

# Common Ground

What do each of these people, places or teams have in common?

1) Trevor Linden, Pavel Bure and Henrik Sedin?
   A) They sit 1-2-3 in Nucks all-time points-per-game percentage, respectively.
   B) They are the only Canucks to win an individual trophy at the NHL Awards.
   C) They sit 1-2-3 in Nucks all-time playoff points, respectively.

2) Steve Tambellini, Ryan Walter and Mike Gillis?
   A) They were all drafted in the first round of the 1978 draft.
   B) According to management, they were the three main candidates for the GM opening after Dave Nonis was fired.
   C) They are all formerly player agents.

3) Mason Raymond, Steve Bernier and Alexandre Burrows?
   A) They all received scholarship offers from the University of Minnesota–Duluth (Raymond was the only one who accepted).
   B) They have all won the Fred J. Hume award, a Canucks trophy for "Unsung Hero."
   C) They all appeared together on the *Late Show with David Letterman* in 2011, to read the "Top 10 Things Americans Don't Know About Hockey."

4) Alex Burrows, Ryan Kesler and Henrik Sedin?
   A) They were the three Canucks nominated for individual awards in 2010–11.
   B) They played the 2008–09 and 2009–10 seasons without missing a single game.
   C) They were the three players Mike Gillis guaranteed would never be traded from the team during his post-season address on May 28, 2011.

5) Pavel Bure and Alexander Mogilny?
   A) They are the only Canucks to score 50+ goals in one season.
   B) They are the only Russians to record more than 50 points for Vancouver.
   C) They are the last players to miss the start of a season due to contract disputes.

· · · · · · · · · · · · · · · · · · · ·

*Roberto Luongo and the rest of Team Canada are the first players to win Olympic gold on home ice. Luongo will likely be the only goalie to ever win it in his home rink.*

**6)** Georges Laraque, Sidney Crosby and Zdeno Chara?

    A) At the 2010 NHL Awards they all received as many votes as Kyle Wellwood did for the Lady Byng, awarded for "sportsmanship and gentlemanly conduct."

    B) Vancouver players in 2011 voted them as the three hardest players to play against.

    C) They all own property in Vancouver.

**7)** Hamilton, Saskatoon and Tokyo?

    A) The Canucks have played regular-season NHL games in all three venues.

    B) An ill-fated promotion for the 1997–98 season brought Canuck stars Pavel Bure and Gino Odjick on a summer speaking tour through these three cities.

    C) According to the official Canucks Fan Club, these locales feature the most fans per-capita of any cities outside of BC.

**8)** Mathieu Schneider, Mike Sillinger, J.J. Daigneault, Michel Petit and Jim Dowd?

    A) All five demanded to be traded from Vancouver.

    B) They are the five Canucks who played the most games without registering a single goal with the club.

    C) They have played with more teams than any other players in NHL history, and all five suited up for Vancouver.

**9)** Markus Naslund, Stan Smyl and Thomas Gradin?

    A) When they retired, all three sat first in Canucks all-time points.

    B) A 2012 poll on Canucks.com found they are the most popular Canucks of all time.

    C) Post retirement, all three expressed interest in a return to the Canucks lineup (though none of them actually made the comeback).

**10)** Calgary, Los Angeles and Edmonton?

    A) The Canucks have the best all-time winning percentage against these three teams.

    B) Over their history, the Canucks have played these teams more than any others.

    C) The Canucks have never won a regular season game in April against these teams.

   • • • • • • • • • • • • • • • • • •

*The 1994–95 Canucks scored 153 goals in a lockout-shortened 48 games, only 39 less goals than the 1998–99 team scored all year.*

# Gone Prospecting

Can you match up the first and last names of these promising Canuck prospects?

| | |
|---|---|
| Adam | Grenier |
| Steven | Corrado |
| Zack | Price |
| Jordan | Gaunce |
| Prab | Kassian |
| Joseph | Rai |
| Patrick | Polasek |
| Frank | Tommernes |
| Anton | Jensen |
| Eddie | McNally |
| Brendan | Schroeder |
| Yann | Ellington |
| Kevin | Rodin |
| Taylor | Lack |
| Jeremy | Labate |
| Nicklas | Anthony |
| Henrik | Connauton |
| Alex | Sauve |

• • • • • • • • • • • • • • • • • •

**Q:** *Two men have won the Jack Adams award for NHL Coach of the Year with the Canucks. Who were they, and what years did they win?*

# Around the Rink Again

The last names of fourteen Canucks are listed. Fill their first names into the grid below, beginning with #1 in the upper left corner. Follow the arrows as you work around – the puzzle winds from the outside into the centre. The last letter from the first name forms the first letter from the second name, and so on.

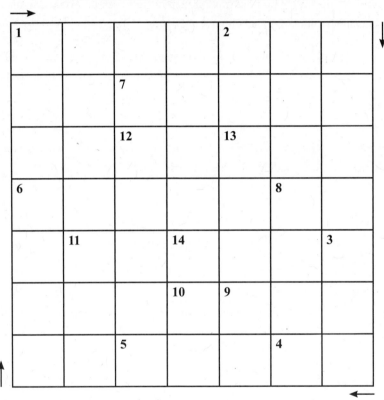

| 1) Schaefer | 6) Baumgartner | 11) Weinrich |
| --- | --- | --- |
| 2) Captain goalie | 7) Petr (last name?) | 12) Neely |
| 3) Vaananen | 8) Gagner | 13) Cooke |
| 4) Boldirev | 9) Jovanovski | 14) Tanti |
| 5) McIver | 10) Babych | |

*362 Canadians have laced up the skates for Vancouver. The most-represented province is Ontario, with 141 players, followed by Alberta with 48, Quebec and BC both with 47, Saskatchewan with 36, Manitoba with 29, and the Atlantic provinces with 14 players combined.*

# Remember Me?

Can you figure out which former Canuck these clues are referring to?

**1)** Hailing from the strong '03 draft, this 16th-overall pick was selected ahead of Zach Parise, Ryan Getzlaf, Mike Richards and Corey Perry. San Jose traded their 21st, 66th and 107th picks to get him at 16th, but would end up trading him midway through his third season. Another trade landed him in Vancouver, and another trade shipped him out in 2010. _____

**2)** This '10 Cup winner played his first six years in Vancouver before being dealt to the Islanders. A couple years later he came back at the trade deadline, but left again after the season. He was traded again later in '10, landing in Atlanta. _____

**3)** This '09 Cup winner was in the spotlight in 2010 for his hit on Marc Savard, which contributed to the "hits to the head" rule change. As a Canuck he scored the tying goal of Game 7 against Calgary in '04 with only 5.2 seconds left, sending GM Place into a short-lived euphoria. _____

**4)** After leaving Vancouver in a trade, this forward had brief stints in Florida, Detroit, Anaheim and Calgary before returning to Detroit again. He never regained the form of his best days in Van, where he scored 0.84 points/game compared with 0.59 points/game elsewhere. _____

**5)** Once traded straight up for Jaromir Jagr, he played a full season with Vancouver in 2005–06, scoring a career-high 33 goals while being named the team's most exciting player. After the season he demanded a higher contract than the Canucks were willing to pay, and only played 64 NHL games after that, recording a mere 28 points. _____

**6)** A former first-round pick, this goalie struggled after leaving Vancouver, posting just six wins in 24 starts the next season before suffering a serious hip injury. He would return for nine NHL games in 2007–08, winning just two games and posting a 3.44 GAA. He was offered a 2009 tryout with Detroit, but did not stick with the club. _____

**7)** After posting 28 points in 41 games (and an additional eight points in eight playoff games) in '09, he announced his retirement the following fall. He leaves the league ranked 25th in all-time points and first in goals, assists and points earned by a Swede. _____

**Q:** *In 2012, which Canuck finished 10th in voting for the Norris Trophy?*

**8)** Leaving Van in '06 (the same year he put a devastating hit on Jaromir Jagr at the Olympics), he has continued to wag his tongue at opponents (figuratively and literally). In his last five seasons he had 81 points and 566 PIMs, and came within two games of the Cup in 2008. He is currently playing in Finland . _____

**9)** After Vancouver he signed with the Rangers as an assistant captain, leading them in goals the next season with 24. Despite signing a two-year deal, he would announce his retirement immediately following the playoffs. He came out of retirement later that year to play with Modo in Sweden, where he recorded 29 points in 29 games, choosing to play the entire season without pay. _____

**10)** Host of the first annual Tofino Saltwater Classic Fishing Derby in 2010, this BC-born player left the Canucks to free agency in 2008. He then played with Anaheim, Dallas and Washington, scoring 73 points over 155 games. Despite attending Canucks camp and showing well in pre-season, he was cut from the team in 2010 and joined Calgary. _____

**11)** This former Sedin linemate found moderate success in his first year after leaving Vancouver, finishing second on his team in plus/minus with +13. Though he has never quite lived up to expectations, this former 8th-overall draft pick ('99) was queitly signed by the Rangers a few weeks before the Nash blockbluster trade. His younger brother Tom currently plays for Tampa, and their father Nelson was an NHLer back in the '70s. _____

**12)** This former defenceman signed a $40-million contract in 2011. His loss was downplayed by Henrik Sedin in the off-season, stating, "I don't think we lost anything. He was in a spot where other guys can step up and take his role." _____

**13)** After some heated dealings with management this player left Vancouver to head south. In 2000–01, he scored 59 goals and 92 points, a full 55 more points than anyone on his team. In fact, he scored 29.5% of his team's total goals. He was traded mid-season to the Rangers, where he finished the season with 20 points in 12 games. Plagued by knee injuries he was forced to retire in '05, and was subsequently named the GM of his country's Olympic team in '06. _____

**14)** After leaving the Canucks this goalie played eight games with Carolina, 37 with Florida and 45 with the Rangers, earning 32 total wins while adapting to a backup role. Since retiring he has served as a goalie coach for the Kamloops Blazers, commentated for Canucks PPV games, and frequently works with the Canucks Alumni group. He currently owns a restaurant in Vancouver and co-owns the BCHL's Burnaby Express. _____

• • • • • • • • • • • • • • • • • • • •

*Q: Only counting their 24 games against Northwest opponents, the 2011-12 Canucks recorded what goal differential?  A) +14  B) +26  C) +35  D) +42*

# SudoClue #4

Each clue below is answered with a number, corresponding to the key below. That number then goes into the two locations listed in brackets. This is a sudoku grid, meaning each row, column and 3x3 grid must have the numbers 1–9 in it only once each. After you've filled in the clues, you'll need to complete the grid according to this rule.
We've filled in a few numbers to start you off.

## KEY

Canuck Winger = **1**        Canuck Goalie = **4**        Canuck Head Coach = **7**
Canuck Centre = **2**        Canuck Broadcaster = **5**        Canuck Owner = **8**
Canuck Defence = **3**        Non-Canuck player = **6**        Millionaires Player = **9**

1) Doug Lidster  [A1, C5]

2) Tom Larscheid  [C6, G8]

3) Daniel Sedin  [C2, E9]

4) Johan Hedberg  [F8, I2]

5) Francesco Aquilini  [E2, G5]

6) Thomas Gradin  [A9, D5]

7) Tom Renney  [D3, G4]

8) Jan Hrdina  [A4, I5]

9) Garth Butcher  [G2, I6]

10) John Shorthouse  [A7, F9]

11) Gary "Suitcase" Smith  [A6, G9]

12) Frank Nighbor  [A2, D9]

13) Mikael Samuelsson  [B6, F5]

14) Arthur Griffiths  [C9, F7]

15) Andrew Cassels  [C4, G1]

16) Fred Taylor  [F1, G6]

17) Mike Keenan  [E8, I9]

18) Bobby Holik  [C1, E6]

• • • • • • • • • • • • • •

*Pavel Bure retired with 437 goals and 779 points in 702 games, adding 70 points in 64 playoff games. He led the league in goal-scoring three times ('94, '00 and '01). Perhaps most impressively, his .622 goals/game is third best among the league's top 100 scorers, trailing only Bossy and Lemieux.*

|   | 1 | 2 | 3 | 4 | 5 | 6 | 7 | 8 | 9 |
|---|---|---|---|---|---|---|---|---|---|
| A |   |   |   |   |   |   |   |   |   |
| B |   |   | 5 |   |   |   | 4 |   |   |
| C |   |   |   |   |   |   |   |   |   |
| D |   |   |   |   |   |   |   | 3 |   |
| E |   |   |   | 9 |   |   |   |   |   |
| F |   |   |   |   |   |   |   |   |   |
| G |   |   |   |   |   |   |   |   |   |
| H |   |   |   |   |   |   |   |   | 6 |
| I | 8 |   |   |   |   |   |   |   |   |

**Q:** *Alex Auld has won 39 games as a Canuck. What position does this put him in all-time Canuck wins?  A) 5th  **B)** 7th  **C)** 10th  **D)** 14th*

# Lost Coaches

The last names of all 16 coaches in Canuck history are hidden below.
As a bonus, can you fill in all their first names?

| W | M | C | C | R | N | A | N | E | E | K | A |
|---|---|---|---|---|---|---|---|---|---|---|---|
| A | L | C | R | E | L | E | A | Q | U | I | T |
| T | A | R | C | L | G | O | I | R | U | Q | L |
| M | C | C | R | A | K | R | T | L | U | M | U |
| W | A | T | T | E | M | E | O | I | S | A | A |
| M | A | L | O | N | N | M | N | F | T | O | E |
| E | F | E | O | B | K | N | O | F | A | N | N |
| O | Y | Y | A | N | Y | L | E | N | S | L | G |
| C | M | C | C | R | E | A | R | Y | I | K | I |
| Y | H | Q | U | I | N | Y | A | L | U | K | V |
| A | C | R | A | W | F | O | R | D | K | F | E |
| L | V | I | G | N | E | N | N | E | R | A | L |

| | | |
|---|---|---|
| CRAWFORD | LEY | QUINN |
| KEENAN | MALONEY | RENNEY |
| KURTENBACH | MCCAMMON | STASIUK |
| LAFORGE | MCCREARY | VIGNEAULT |
| LAYCOE | NEALE | WATT |
| | NEILSON | |

· · · · · · · · · · · · · · · · · ·

**Q:** *The Canucks were eliminated by the Chicago Blackhawks for two straight years on the exact same day. What day is it?*

# Scrambled Rookies

All of these players made their NHL debuts between 2005 and 2012, with the Canucks. Can you unscramble them all? Watch out, an extra letter has been added to each name to throw you off.

1) Arandeexl Crudlob _____

2) Lamerich Brenrag _____

3) Clua Durnboo _____

4) Riches Veant _____

5) Docty Snogdoh _____

6) Nomast Drymoan _____

7) Leed Tweast _____

8) Krice Priney _____

9) Vintek Abekis _____

10) Randleexa Reeldy _____

11) Nikonaj Sheann _____

12) Haanten Crimev _____

13) Rocya Scidreehn _____

14) Ramoin Nabzkil _____

15) Balil Twaset _____

16) Grisee Vookhirsz _____

• • • • • • • • • • • • • • • • • • • • • •

**Q:** *How many years did Jim Robson do play-by-play for Canuck radio broadcasts?*
*A) 10  B) 16  C) 20  D) 24  Who succeeded him in this role?*

# Last Choice

1) Tiger Williams was suspended for one playoff game in 1980 for allegedly hitting whom with his stick? The play was not captured by any cameras.
   A) Scotty Bowman, the coach of the Buffalo Sabres at the time.
   B) Pat O'Hall, a linesman.
   C) A fan of the Calgary Flames.

2) Alexander Mogilny was the first...
   A) Canuck to record a playoff hat trick, doing so in 1996 against Colorado.
   B) Russian to defect from the old Soviet Union to play in the NHL.
   C) Canuck to shoot the puck over 400 times in a single season (he did it 411 times in 1995–96).

3) Played after every Chicago goal, what song would most Canuck fans and players refer to as their most hated?
   A) "Chelsea Dagger," The Fratellis
   B) "O Fortuna," Carl Orff
   C) "Click Click Boom," Saliva
   D) "You're the Inspiration," Chicago

4) The Canucks switched in 2011-12 to which goal song?.
   A) U2 – "Elevation"
   B) Clutch – "Electric Worry"
   C) System of a Down – "Chop Suey"
   D) Green Day – "Holiday"

5) When was the last home game not counted as a sellout?
   A) November 9, 2000 vs. Los Angeles
   B) November 12, 2002 vs. St. Louis
   C) January 6, 2004 vs. Nashville
   D) December 11, 2005 vs. Minnesota

• • • • • • • • • • • • • • • • • • • •

*In the voting for the 2008 Selke Award, Ryan Kesler finished 11th. The next year he finished third. In 2010, he trailed Pavel Datsyuk by just one first-place vote. In 2011, he finally took the trophy home, beating second-place by a definitive 703 votes.*

**6)** Which three are Hall of Famers who suited up for the Canucks?
  A) Pavel Bure, Mark Messier and Pat Quinn
  B) Mark Messier, Cam Neely and Igor Larionov
  C) Mark Messier, Alex Mogilny and Ivan Hlinka
  D) Mark Messier, Cam Neely and Glenn Anderson

**7)** What strange injury caused Brent Sopel to miss the '07 playoff opener vs Dallas?
  A) He injured his back bending down to pick up a cracker from the floor.
  B) He injured his pinky finger typing on a computer.
  C) He ruptured his eardrum with a Q-tip.
  D) He cut his neck with a pair of scissors while attempting to self-style his mullet.

**8)** Which three players combined for more points?
  A) Andre Boudrias, Don Lever and John Gould in 1974–75.
  B) Pavel Bure, Cliff Ronning and Greg Adams in 1992–93.
  C) Markus Naslund, Todd Bertuzzi and Brendan Morrison in 2002–03.
  D) Henrik Sedin, Daniel Sedin and Alex Burrows in 2010–11.

**9)** In Roberto Luongo's first season with the Canucks...
  A) He posted a Canucks-record 47 wins, one win off Martin Brodeur's NHL record.
  B) He played in 76 of 82 games, posting a 2.28 GAA and .921 save percentage.
  C) He led the Canucks to a quadruple-OT win over Dallas, saving 72 of a playoff record 76 shots in the sixth-longest game ever.
  D) All of the above.

**10)** Jan Bulis is perhaps best remembered for an odd play during a February 25, 2007 game against Dallas. What happened?
  A) He hopped onto a Stars player for a piggyback ride into the offensive zone, and a few seconds later tried to cut between goalie and the net, leading to a well-deserved interference penalty.
  B) He mistook the referee for a Stars' defencemen, hooking him as the ref skated into the defensive zone.
  C) A strap on his pants broke off after blocking a shot, causing them to fall down around his ankles as he skated towards the bench.

· · · · · · · · · · · · · · · · · · · · · · · ·

*Frank Patrick, co-founder of the Pacific Coast Hockey Association along with his brother Lester, was instrumental in bringing Vancouver the 1915 Stanley Cup. He served as team coach, manager, president, owner and defenceman. He was inducted into the Hall of Fame as a builder in 1958.*

# Another Numbers Game

Using the numbers in the box below, can you fill in all these clues about the Canucks?
Cross out the numbers as you go. Each is only used once.

1) # of teams in the league for Vancouver's first season _____

2) # of teams in the league for Vancouver's 40th season _____

3) # of seconds it took Ryan Walter, Sergio Momesso and Trevor Linden to score the three fastest goals in team history _____

4) # of career points Linden scored against Edmonton (the most any Canuck has ever scored against another team) _____

5) # of NHL seasons Trevor Linden played _____

6) # of consecutive games Linden played, ending in 1996 _____

7) Record # of consecutive games Iron Man Brendan Morrison played _____

8) # of players who appeared for at least one game in Canucks history _____

9) # of players with 100+ games in Canuck history _____

10) # of players with 500+ games in Canuck history _____

11) # of players with at least one playoff game in Canuck history _____

12) # of players with 100+ playoff games in Canuck history _____

13) # of millions of dollars Mats Sundin was originally offered per year _____

14) Roberto Luongo's age when he joined Vancouver _____

15) Roberto Luongo's age when his current contract will expire _____

16) # of regular season goals scored by Vancouver _____

17) # of regular season goals allowed by Vancouver _____

| 1 | 25 | 48 | 260 | 534 |
| 10 | 27 | 76 | 482 | 10,366 |
| 14 | 30 | 186 | 512 | 11,012 |
| 22 | 43 | | | |

• • • • • • • • • • • • • • • • • • • •

**Q:** *As of 2012, the Canucks will have retired three players' numbers officially, and another one unofficially (in '74, though this was later unretired).*
*Who were the players and their numbers?*

# Hometown Heroes

Can you match these Canuck fan favourites with their hometowns?
Listed beside each is their best single-season totals with Vancouver.

| | |
|---|---|
| Richard Brodeur | Glendon, Alberta (88 pts in 74 games) |
| Tiger Williams | Medicine Hat, Alberta (80 pts in 82 games) |
| Gino Odjick | Willowdale, Ontario (2.29 playoff GAA) |
| Alex Burrows | Montreal, Quebec (2.52 playoff GAA) |
| Tony Tanti | Longueuil, Quebec (2.70 playoff GAA) |
| Trevor Linden | Pitea, Sweden (+16, 36 pts) |
| Thomas Gradin | Toronto, Ontario (45 goals, 86 points) |
| Markus Naslund | Ornskoldsvik, Sweden (48 goals, 105 points) |
| Jyrki Lumme | Maniwaki, Quebec (+13, 16 goals, 271 PIMs) |
| Mattias Ohlund | Windsor, Ontario (+19, 46 pts in 67 games) |
| Henrik Sedin | Edmonton, Alberta (+22, 17 pts) |
| Ryan Kesler | Moscow, Russia (+35, 60 goals, 110 pts) |
| Pavel Bure | Solleftea, Sweden (37 goals, 86 pts, 19 playoff pts) |
| Cliff Ronning | Weyburn, Sasketchewan (35 goals, 62 pts, 343 PIMs) |
| Ed Jovanovski | Livonia, Michigan (75 pts, 10 playoff pts) |
| Stan Smyl | Burnaby, BC (29 goals, 85 pts) |
| Kirk McLean | Pincourt, Quebec (+34, 35 goals, 67 pts) |
| Harold Snepsts | Tampere, Finland (+30, 55 pts in 74 games) |
| Roberto Luongo | Ornskoldsvik, Sweden (+35, 112 pts) |

• • • • • • • • • • • • • • • • • • • • •

*Sedin-Off: Henrik has 146 more penalty minutes than Daniel. Hank has taken 900 less shots than Daniel (who has fired 2,223 pucks). Daniel has 60 game-winners to Henrik's 32, but Henrik has 29 more total points, entirely due to his 33 more games played.*

# Answers

## The Team, Pages 4–5

1) Carolina: USA
2) Florida: USA
3) Van: Canada
4) Van: Canada
5) Florida: USA
6) Van: Sweden
7) Florida: USA
8) Van: Canada
9) Nashville: Canada
10) Van: Denmark
11) Anaheim: Canada
12) Florida: Canada
13) Van: USA
14) Florida: Canada
15) San Jose: Canada
16) Florida: Canada
17) Van: Denmark
18) Van: Canada
19) Van: Canada
20) Columbus: Canada
21) Buffalo: Canada
22) Ottawa: Finland
23) Van: Canada
24) Van: USA
25) Van: Sweden
26) Van: Sweden
27) Van: USA
28) Van: Canada

## Around the Rink, Page 6

1) Jyrki
2) Igor
3) Richard
4) Dave
5) Evan
6) Neil
7) Luc
8) Cliff
9) Fedor
10) Russ
11) Steve
12) Esa
13) Artem
14) Mats

## Draft Day, Page 7

1) A: other teams thought he wasn't draft eligible yet, and after nearly a year-long battle the Canucks were able to keep their star pick.
2) A
3) C
4) B
5) B
6) A

A: Kurtenbach (70–74), Boudrias (75–76), Oddleif-son (76–77), Lever (77–79), McCarthy (79–82), Smyl (82–90), Quinn, Lidster & Linden (91–90 tri-captains), Linden (91–97), Messier (97–00), Naslund (00–08), Luongo (08–10), Sedin (10–)

## '70s, '80s, '90s or '00s, Page 8

1) 1997
2) 1998
3) 1993
4) 2001
5) 1995
6) 1992
7) 2007
8) 2001
9) 1975
10) 1982
11) 1993
12) 1999
13) 1979
14) 1984
15) 1982

A: Mikael Samuelsson: he won the Cup in '08 with Detroit, and played with Sweden for the '06 Olympic Gold in Turin and the '06 IIHF World Championship.

## Nicknames, Page 9

Mayday: Brad May
Russian Rocket: Pavel Bure
Steamer: Stan Smyl
Bloodbank: Wade Brookbank
The Brabarian: Jeff Cowan
Captain Canuck: Trevor Linden
Captain Kirk: Kirk McLean
Frankenswede: Mats Sundin
The Moose: Mark Messier
Crouton: Vladimir Krutov
Jovocop: Ed Jovanovski
The Sandman: Curtis Sanford
The Strangler: Garth Butcher
The House: Jim Sandlak
Juice: Kevin Bieksa
Bill Pickle: Willie Mitchell
Bobby Lou: Roberto Luongo

A: 1) Alexander Mogilny  2) Bob Essensa
   3) Todd Bertuzzi  4) Richard Brodeur
   5) Rick Rypien  6) Cody Hodgson
   7) Brendan Morrison

## Opening Night, Pages 10–11

| Across | Down |
|---|---|
| 1) Hodgson | 1) Homer |
| 5) Smyl | 2) Draft |
| 9) Miami | 3) NHL |
| 10) Green | 4) Skills |
| 11) Don | 6) Marc |
| 12) Tyler | 7) Trent |
| 16) Rypien | 8) Andre |
| 19) Sabres | 13) Robson |
| 21) Flames | 14) Griffiths |
| 22) LA | 15) Gus |
| 23) Millionaires | 17) Place |
| 26) Harold | 18) Naslund |
| 28) Sedin | 20) Reid |
| 30) Malik | 23) Moose |
| 32) Alternate | 24) Lord |
| | 25) Four |
| | 27) Rome |
| | 29) Net |
| | 31) KO |

**A:** Henrik Sedin (21st), Daniel Sedin (t-28th), Chris Higgins (t-35th), Sami Salo (t-44th) and Manny Malhotra (t-46th).

## A Numbers Game, Page 12

| | |
|---|---|
| 1) 41 | 10) 943 |
| 2) 25 | 11) 18 |
| 3) 16 | 12) 406 |
| 4) 219 | 13) 18,860 |
| 5) 346 | 14) 16,281 |
| 6) 192 | 15) 746,900 |
| 7) 117 | 16) 1,050,000 |
| 8) 48 | 17) 3,133,000 |
| 9) 2,326 | 18) 8,700,000 |

**A:** Ryan Kesler

## Your Choice, Pages 13–14

| | |
|---|---|
| 1) C | 6) A |
| 2) A | 7) B |
| 3) B | 8) C |
| 4) A | 9) A |
| 5) B | 10) D |

## The Run, Page 15

1) Boston
2) San Jose
3) Boston
4) Boston
5) Chicago
6) San Jose
7) Nashville
8) Nashville
9) Chicago
10) San Jose
11) Boston
12) Boston
13) Boston
14) Chicago

## SudoClue, Pages 16–17

| 2 | 5 | 4 | 6 | 3 | 8 | 7 | 1 | 9 |
|---|---|---|---|---|---|---|---|---|
| 6 | 7 | 9 | 4 | 1 | 2 | 3 | 8 | 5 |
| 1 | 8 | 3 | 5 | 9 | 7 | 4 | 6 | 2 |
| 8 | 3 | 7 | 9 | 6 | 4 | 2 | 5 | 1 |
| 5 | 9 | 6 | 3 | 2 | 1 | 8 | 4 | 7 |
| 4 | 2 | 1 | 7 | 8 | 5 | 6 | 9 | 3 |
| 3 | 4 | 5 | 1 | 7 | 6 | 9 | 2 | 8 |
| 7 | 1 | 8 | 2 | 4 | 9 | 5 | 3 | 6 |
| 9 | 6 | 2 | 8 | 5 | 3 | 1 | 7 | 4 |

**First Round Search, Page 18**

Over one Canuck game: Allen, Bourdon, Grabner, Hodgson, Holden, Kesler, Linden, Nedved, Ohlund, Schneider, D. Sedin, H. Sedin, Smith, Stojanov, Woodley

Over 100 NHL Games: Allen, Ference, Grabner Kesler, Linden, Nedved, Ohlund, D. Sedin, H. Sedin, Stojanov, Umberger, Wilson.

**A:** Markus Naslund: Five
Pavel Bure: Four
Ed Jovanovski: Three
Roberto Luongo: Three
Henrik Sedin: Three

**Down the Centre, Page 19**

1) N (Brendan Morrison)
2) Y (Ryan Kesler)
3) B (Artem Chubarov)
4) D (Cody Hodgson)
5) M (Thomas Gradin)
6) M (Mark Messier)
7) D (Harold Druken)
8) S (Andrew Cassels)
9) L (Mike Sillinger)
10) D (Barry Pederson)
11) I (Igor Larionov)
12) L (Nathan Lafayette)
13) C (Dave Scatchard)
14) L (Kyle Wellwood)
15) L (Manny Malhotra)
16) P (Maxim Lapierre)

**A:** East (1970–74), Smythe (1974–93), Pacific (1993–98), Northwest (1998–present)

**Path to the Big Leagues, Pages 20–21**

1) Zack Kassian
2) Rick Rypien
3) Roberto Luongo
4) Keith Ballard
5) Ryan Kesler
6) Mason Raymond
7) David Booth
8) Alexander Edler
9) Chris Higgins
10) Alex Burrows
11) Henrik Sedin
12) Daniel Sedin
13) Dan Hamhuis

**Notable Names, Page 22**

Stan Smyl: First Canuck to 200 goals
Mike Gillis: General manager
Nathan Lafayette: Hit post in Game 7
Mike Burnstein: Head athletic trainer
Cyclone Taylor: Vancouver Millionaires star
Mark Donnelly: Current anthem singer
Barry Wilkins: Scored first Canucks goal
Richard Loney: Former anthem singer
Ron Delorme: Chief scout
Pat O'Neill: Equipment manager
Trevor Linden: First Canuck to 300 goals
Andre Boudrias: First Canuck to 100 goals
John Ashbridge: Public address announcer
Francesco Aquilini: Owner
Orland Kurtenbach: First captain
Rory Fitzpatrick: Almost '07 All-Star
Dale Tallon: First-ever draft pick

## P's and Q's, Page 23

1) Brown (Cam, Jeff, Mike, Mike and Sean)
2) Daniel and Henrik Sedin
   Geoff and Russ Courtnall
   Jack and Dave Capuano
3) X and U
4) B
5) Sami Salo
   Andrew Alberts
   Manny Malhotra
6) Sheldon Kannegiesser

**A:** Keith Ballard accidentally hit Tomas Vokoun on November 20, 2009.

## SudoClue #2, Pages 24–25

| 2 | 5 | 6 | 8 | 3 | 7 | 1 | 9 | 4 |
|---|---|---|---|---|---|---|---|---|
| 4 | 9 | 7 | 2 | 6 | 1 | 3 | 5 | 8 |
| 3 | 8 | 1 | 4 | 5 | 9 | 6 | 2 | 7 |
| 8 | 7 | 4 | 5 | 1 | 2 | 9 | 3 | 6 |
| 6 | 3 | 5 | 9 | 4 | 8 | 7 | 1 | 2 |
| 9 | 1 | 2 | 3 | 7 | 6 | 4 | 8 | 5 |
| 1 | 6 | 8 | 7 | 2 | 3 | 5 | 4 | 9 |
| 7 | 4 | 9 | 1 | 8 | 5 | 2 | 6 | 3 |
| 5 | 2 | 3 | 6 | 9 | 4 | 8 | 7 | 1 |

**A:** Referee Stephane Auger. Burrows was fined $25,000 for his comments, and Auger hasn't worked the Canucks (or the playoffs) since.

## Line Change, Page 26

1) A: 2009–10
2) C: 1997–98
3) B: 2007–08
4) B: 2006–07
5) C: 1981–82
6) D: 2005–06

## Fill Me In, Page 27

1) '01: Trent Klatt & Todd Bertuzzi
   '02: Trent Klatt
   '03: Trent Klatt & Trevor Linden
   '04: Jason King & Magnus Arvedson
   '06: Anson Carter
   '07: Taylor Pyatt
   '08: Taylor Pyatt & Markus Naslund
   '09: Alex Burrows & Pavol Demitra & Steve Bernier
   '10: Alex Burrows & Mikael Samuelsson
2) '07: Dany Sabourin
   '08: Curtis Sanford
   '09: Curtis Sanford & Jason LaBarbera
   '10: Andrew Raycroft
   '11–'12: Cory Schneider

3) Calgary, Colorado, Edmonton & Minnesota
4) 1: Roberto Luongo, 2: Henrik Sedin, 3: Daniel Sedin, 4: Ryan Kesler

## True or False, Pages 28–29

1) True
2) True
3) True
4) False
5) True
6) False
7) True (lockout year)
8) True
9) True
10) True
11) False
12) False
13) True
14) False
15) True
16) False

**A:** Trevor Linden

## Road Trip, Page 30

| | |
|---|---|
| 1) 42 | 10) 30 |
| 2) 14 | 11) 6 |
| 3) 13 | 12) 22,235 |
| 4) 20,737 | 13) 12,861 |
| 5) 8 | 14) 47 |
| 6) 5 | 15) 45 |
| 7) 1 | 16) 10 |
| 8) 2 | 17) 300 |
| 9) 3 | 18) 11 |

**A:** 1) Henrik Sedin (6)
  2) Kevin Bieksa (24:46)
  3) Maxim Lapierre (16)
  4) Zack Kassian (+1) *He was the only Canuck with a positive plus/minus
  5) Manny Malhotra (64.6%)
  6) Kevin Bieksa (1)

## Goalie Graveyard, Page 31

1) Felix Potvin
2) Garth Snow
3) Corey Schwab
4) Kevin Weekes
5) Corey Hirsch
6) Artus Irbe
7) Alex Auld
8) Dan Cloutier
9) Maxime Ouellet
10) Mika Noronen
11) Johan Hedberg
12) Peter Skudra
13) Martin Brochu
14) Bob Essensa
15) Sean Burke

**A:** 1) Sedins and Jason King (two twins & a king)
  2) Sedins and Naslund
  3) Naslund, Morrison and Bertuzzi
  4) Sedins and Anson Carter
  5) Linden, Ronning and Courtnall

## The Trade, Pages 32–33

1) Pittsburgh; Alex Stojanov
2) Boston; Cam Neely
3) Todd Bertuzzi, Bryan McCabe, 3rd-round pick ('98); NY Islanders
4) Brad Lukowich, Christian Ehrhoff
5) Matt Cooke
6) Roberto Luongo, Lukas Krajicek, 6th-round pick ('06); Florida
7) Cliff Ronning, Sergio Momesso, Geoff Courtnall
8) New Jersey; Alexander Mogilny
9) Ottawa; Peter Schaefer
10) Richard Brodeur
11) Ed Jovanovski, Dave Gagner, Kevin Weekes, Mike Brown, con. 1st-round pick; Pavel Bure
12) Buffalo; 3rd ('09) and 2nd-round ('10) picks
13) Keith Ballard, Victor Oreskovich; Michael Grabner, 1st-round pick ('10)
14) Dan Cloutier
15) Washington

## Faceoff, Pages 34–35

| Across | Down |
|---|---|
| 1) Neely | 1) Northwest |
| 4) American | 2) Hip |
| 6) Robson | 3) Pat |
| 11) Hockey | 5) Mattias |
| 12) Thomas | 7) Backup |
| 14) Salo | 8) Overtime |
| 15) Points | 9) Jovo |
| 17) Ads | 10) Dave |
| 18) Todd | 13) Russian |
| 19) Mike | 14) Steve |
| 21) Leftwing | 16) Odjick |
| 24) Men | 19) Motors |
| 26) Lockout | 20) Kick |
| 28) Nike | 21) Lou |
| 29) Salmon Kings | 22) Tanti |
| | 23) GM |
| | 25) Edge |
| | 27) Ten |

## More Choice, Pages 36–37

| | |
|---|---|
| 1) C | 6) D |
| 2) A | 7) C |
| 3) C | 8) A |
| 4) B | 9) A |
| 5) D | 10) B |

**A:** B (10 games)

## Word Work, Page 38

### Vancouver

| | | | |
|---|---|---|---|
| Ace | Cornea | Once | Rune |
| Aeon | Cove | One | Uncover |
| Aero | Cover | Orc | Urea |
| Acne | Crane | Orca | Urn |
| Acorn | Crave | Ore | Van |
| Acre | Crone | Ounce | Vane |
| Arc | Cue | Our | Vena |
| Are | Cure | Ova | |
| Can | Curve | Oven | |
| Cane | Ear | Over | |
| Canoe | Earn | Race | |
| Car | Eon | Ran | |
| Care | Era | Rave | |
| Carve | Euro | Raven | |
| Cave | Narc | Rev | |
| Cavern | Nave | Roan | |
| Con | Near | Roc | |
| Cone | Nor | Rove | |
| Core | Nova | Rue | |
| Corn | Ocean | Run | |

### Canucks

| | | | |
|---|---|---|---|
| Ankus | Can | Sack | Snuck |
| Anus | Cask | Sank | Suck |
| Ask | Cusk | Ska | Sun |
| Auk | Sac | Snack | Sunk |

**A:** True

## Spot the Fakes, Page 39

1) Steven Pen and Red Brown
2) Randy Quick and Radulan Hrzck
3) The Corner and Bagel
4) Bakkenfraz and Lose

**A:** Marc Crawford (six seasons)
　　Alain Vigneault (2011–12 is sixth season)

## Playoff Puzzle, Page 40-41

1) D
2) A
3) B (Philly over Boston in 2010 quarterfinals, Islanders
　　over Pens in 1975 quarterfinals, Leafs over Red
　　Wings in 1942 Stanley Cup Finals)
4) B
5) C
6) D
7) C
8) D (Henrik finished second (22), Daniel fourth (20),
　　Kesler seventh (19) and Burrows ninth (17).

**A:** D (Hughson has called the Finals since 2009.)

## Top 20 Search, Page 42

| | |
|---|---|
| Greg Adams | Brendan Morrison |
| Todd Bertuzzi | Markus Naslund |
| Andre Boudrias | Mattias Ohlund |
| Pavel Bure | Cliff Ronning |
| Thomas Gradin | Daniel Sedin |
| Dennis Kearns | Henrik Sedin |
| Don Lever | Petri Skriko |
| Trevor Linden | Stan Smyl |
| Jyrki Lumme | Patrik Sundstrom |
| Alexander Mogilny | Tony Tanti |

**A:** See next page.

**A:** #1 Naslund (756)
#2 H. Sedin (747)
#3 Linden (733)
#4 D. Sedin (718)
#5 Smyl (673)
#6 Gradin (550)
#7 Bure (478)
#8 Tanti (470)
#9 Bertuzzi (449)
#10 Lever (407)
#11 Morrison (393)
#12 Boudrias (388)
#13 Skriko (373)
#14 Adams (369)
#15 Sundstrom (342)
#16 Kesler (337)
#17 Ronning (328)
#18 Ohlund (325)
#19 Lumme (321)
#20 Kearns (321)

## Canuck Killers, Page 43

1) Joe Sakic
2) Wayne Gretzky
3) Milan Hejduk
4) Andrew Brunette
5) Adam Deadmarsh
6) Teemu Selanne
7) Curtis Sanford
8) Marty Turco
9) Wes Walz
10) Kristian Huselius
11) Peter Forsberg
12) Jarret Stoll
13) Theo Fleury
14) Christian Backman
15) Mark Messier

## Quotables, Pages 44–45

1) A
2) A
3) B (Mikael went on to score a career-high 30 goals, second among all Swedes. His country did not fare so well, finishing fifth at the Games.)
4) A
5) C
6) A
7) B
8) A
9) C

## SudoClue #3, Pages 46–47

| 7 | 2 | 1 | 5 | 9 | 8 | 6 | 3 | 4 |
|---|---|---|---|---|---|---|---|---|
| 3 | 6 | 4 | 2 | 7 | 1 | 9 | 5 | 8 |
| 8 | 9 | 5 | 4 | 3 | 6 | 2 | 1 | 7 |
| 5 | 7 | 8 | 1 | 2 | 4 | 3 | 6 | 9 |
| 9 | 3 | 6 | 8 | 5 | 7 | 1 | 4 | 2 |
| 1 | 4 | 2 | 3 | 6 | 9 | 7 | 8 | 5 |
| 4 | 1 | 3 | 9 | 8 | 2 | 5 | 7 | 6 |
| 2 | 8 | 7 | 6 | 1 | 5 | 4 | 9 | 3 |
| 6 | 5 | 9 | 7 | 4 | 3 | 8 | 2 | 1 |

## Line Change #2, Page 48

1) D
2) B
3) A
4) A
5) C
6) C

**A:** False. The Dallas Stars did it in 1997–98 and 1998–99

## '70s, '80s, '90s or '00s #2, Page 49

1) 1991 (November 5)
2) 2003 (March 15)
3) 1975
4) 1982
5) 1993 (Pavel Bure)
6) 1992
7) 1988
8) 1991
9) 1989
10) 1990
11) 2007
12) 2003 (Markus Naslund)
13) 1978
14) 1989
15) 1997

## Ever a Canuck?, Page 50

1) Curt Giles
2) Lorne "Gump" Worsley
3) John Vanbiesbrouck
4) Owen Nolan
5) Steve Sullivan
6) Brad Ference
7) Lee Stempniak
8) Roger Neilson
9) Ian White
10) Manny Legace
11) Steve Begin
12) Valeri Bure

**A:** Donald Brashear set the record in 1997–98.
(Dave Schultz posted the NHL record
in 1974–75 with 472.)

## Up the Middle, Page 51

1) M (Sami Salo)
2) M (Dan Hamhuis)
3) I (Mattias Ohlund)
4) U (Doug Lidster)
5) J (Lukas Krajicek
6) R (Brent Sopel)
7) L (Bryan Allen)
8) N (Chris Tanev)
9) H (Keith Ballard)
10) C (Dave Babych)
11) I (Willie Mitchell)
12) A (Marek Malik)
13) N (Bryan McCabe)
14) D (Bret Hedican)
15) R (Jason Garrison)
16) N (Dana Murzyn)
17) B (Andrew Alberts)

## In the Crease, Pages 52–53

| Across | Down |
|--------|------|
| 1) Hart | 2) Towel |
| 3) Twins | 3) Tie |
| 7) Taylor | 4) Stan Smyl |
| 9) Sweep | 5) All |
| 11) Knob | 6) Brad |
| 13) Neilson | 8) Sundstrom |
| 16) Sutter | 10) Pond |
| 18) Bryan | 12) Brendan |
| 19) Dave | 14) Inter |
| 20) Rory | 15) Alexander |
| 22) Trip | 17) Retired |
| 24) OT | 21) OT |
| 25) Round | 23) Pre |
| 27) Garage | 26) Deal |
| 30) Donald | 28) Goal |
| 32) Ohlund | 29) SH |
| 33) Glass | 30) Dust |
| 34) Florida | 32) Off |
|  | 33) GA |

**A:** Mason Raymond

## Common Ground, Pages 54–55

1) C (Linden 95, H.Sedin 71, Bure 66)
2) A (Tambellini went on to play 553 games, including 161 with Vancouver. Gillis played 246 games, while Walter enjoyed 1,003 games. He ended his career with Vancouver.)
3) B
4) B
5) A (Bure did it three times. Naslund and Bertuzzi came close in 2002–03, with 48 and 46, respectively).
6) A (they all received one vote)
7) A
8) C
9) A
10) A

## Gone Prospecting, Page 56

Adam Polasek
Steven Anthony
Zack Kassian
Jordan Schroeder
Prab Rai
Joseph Labate
Patrick McNally
Frank Corrado
Anton Rodin
Eddie Lack
Brendan Gaunce
Yann Sauve
Kevin Connauton
Taylor Ellington
Jeremy Price
Nicklas Jensen
Henrik Tommernes
Alex Grenier

A: Pat Quinn in 1993 and Alain Vigneault in 2007

## Around the Rink Again, Page 57

1) Peter
2) Roberto
3) Ossi
4) Ivan
5) Nathan
6) Nolan
7) Nedved
8) Dave
9) Ed
10) Dave
11) Eric
12) Cam
13) Matt
14) Tony

## Remember Me? Pages 58–59

1) Steve Bernier
2) Brent Sopel
3) Matt Cooke
4) Todd Bertuzzi
5) Anson Carter
6) Dan Cloutier
7) Mats Sundin
8) Jarkko Ruutu
9) Markus Naslund
10) Brendan Morrison
11) Taylor Pyatt
12) Christian Ehrhoff
13) Pavel Bure
14) Kirk McLean

A: Christian Ehrhoff

D: They finished +42 against the Northwest

## SudoClue #4, Pages 60–61

| 3 | 9 | 8 | 6 | 7 | 4 | 5 | 1 | 2 |
|---|---|---|---|---|---|---|---|---|
| 7 | 2 | 5 | 8 | 9 | 1 | 4 | 6 | 3 |
| 6 | 1 | 4 | 2 | 3 | 5 | 7 | 9 | 8 |
| 1 | 5 | 7 | 4 | 2 | 8 | 6 | 3 | 9 |
| 4 | 8 | 3 | 9 | 5 | 6 | 2 | 7 | 1 |
| 9 | 6 | 2 | 3 | 1 | 7 | 8 | 4 | 5 |
| 2 | 3 | 6 | 7 | 8 | 9 | 1 | 5 | 4 |
| 5 | 7 | 9 | 1 | 4 | 2 | 3 | 8 | 6 |
| 8 | 4 | 1 | 5 | 6 | 3 | 9 | 2 | 7 |

A: Alex Auld sits 7th with 39 wins. He trails Glen Hanlon (43), Gary Smith (72), Dan Cloutier (109), Richard Brodeur (126), Kirk McLean (211) and Roberto Luongo (224).

## Lost Coaches, Page 62

Marc Crawford
Mike Keenan
Orland Kurtenbach
Bill LaForge
Hal Laycoe
Rick Ley
Phil Maloney
Bob McCammon
Bill McCreary
Harry Neale
Roger Neilson
Pat Quinn
Tom Renney
Vic Stasiuk
Alain Vigneault
Tom Watt

**A:** May 11th (2009 and 2010)

## Scrambled Rookies, Page 63

1) Alexandre Bolduc
2) Michael Grabner
3) Luc Bourdon
4) Mike Brown
5) Jason Jaffray
6) Mason Raymond
7) Evan Oberg
8) Rick Rypien
9) Kevin Bieksa
10) Alexander Edler
11) Jannik Hansen
12) Nathan McIver
13) Cory Schneider
14) Mario Bliznak
15) Bill Sweatt
16) Sergei Shirokov

**A:** D (24 years). He was succeeded by Jim Hughson.

## Last Choice, Pages 64–65

1) A
2) B
3) A
4) B
5) B
6) B
7) A
8) C (272 points)
9) D
10) A

## Another Numbers Game, Page 66

1) 14
2) 30
3) 48
4) 76
5) 22
6) 482
7) 534
8) 512
9) 186
10) 25
11) 260
12) 1 (Linden, 118 games)
13) 10
14) 27
15) 43
16) 10,366
17) 11,012

**A:** Stan Smyl's #12, Trevor Linden's #16, Markus Naslund's #19, Wayne Maki's #11 (later unretired)

## Hometown Heroes, Page 67

Brodeur: Longueuil
Williams: Weyburn
Odjick: Maniwaki
Burrows: Pincourt
Tanti: Toronto
Linden: Medicine Hat
Gradin: Solleftea
Naslund: Ornskoldsvik (105 pts)
Lumme: Tampere
Ohlund: Pitea
Sedin: Ornskoldsvik (112 pts)
Kesler: Livonia
Bure: Moscow
Ronning: Burnaby
Jovanovski: Windsor
Smyl: Glendon
McLean: Willowdale
Snepsts: Edmonton
Luongo: Montreal

# The Puzzling Sports Institute
### www.puzzlingsports.com

**The Puzzling Sports Institute** is the brainchild of **Jesse Ross**, who has loved sports for as long as he can remember. He is the author of the bestselling *O Canada Puzzles for Kids* series and has published four successful books as part of the All-Star Sports Puzzles series as well as the recent *Slapshot Hockey Quizbook*. His puzzles have been published in various newspapers across the US and Canada. Ross lives in the Okanagan.

### Slapshot Hockey Quizbook
*7¼ x 9, 80 pages, paper • 978-0-88971-234-8 • $8.95*

### O Canada Puzzles for Kids
*7½ x 9, 72 pp, pb • 978-1-894404-06-8 • $9.95 • Ages 8 and up*

### O Canada Puzzles for Kids 2
*7½ x 9, 72 pp, pb • 978-1-894404-15-0 • $9.95 • Ages 8 and up*

**ALL AVAILABLE FROM HARBOUR PUBLISHING • www.harbourpublishing.com**